Using Literature in

Your K–4 Classroom:

Practical Ideas for Teachers

Using Literature

in Your K–4 Classroom:

Practical Ideas for Teachers

Barbara Nypaver Kupetz

Christopher-Gordon Publishers, Inc.
Norwood, Massachusetts

Copyright Acknowledgments

Excerpt from Thank You, Mr. Falker by Patricia Polacco. Copyright © 1998 by Babushka, Inc. Used by permission of Philomel Books, a division of Penguin Putnam Inc.

Excerpt from The Library by Sarah Stewart, pictures by David Small. text copyright © 1995 by Sarah Stewart. Illustration copyright 1995 by David Small. Reprinted by permission of Farrar, Straus, and Giroux, LLC.

Excerpt from The Wednesday Surprise by Eve Bunting. Copyright © 1989 by Eve Bunting. Reprinted by permission of Clarion Books/ Houghton Mifflin Company. All rights reserved.

Excerpt from Tikki Tikki Tembo by Arlene Mosel, copyright © 1968 by Arlene Mosel. Reprinted by permission of Henry Holt & Company., LLC.

Excerpt from The Bee Tree by Patricia Polacco. Copyright © 1993 by Patricia Polacco. Used by permission of Philomel Books, a division of Penguin Putnam Inc.

Excerpt from Teaching Reading with Children's Literature, by Cox/Zarillo, copyright © 1993. Adapted by permission of Prentice-Hall, Inc. Upper Saddle River, NJ.

All student work used by permission of parent or guardian.

Every effort has been made to contact copyright holders for permission to reproduce borrowed material where necessary. We apologize for any oversights and would be happy to rectify them in future printings.

The Bill Harp Professional Teacher's Library
An Imprint of
Christopher-Gordon Publishers, Inc.
1502 Providence Highway, Suite 12
Norwood, MA 02062
800-934-8322

Printed in the United States of America

10 9 8 7 6 5 4 3 2 1   05 04 03 02 01 00
Library of Congress Catalog Card Number: 99076805
ISBN: 1-929024-14-2

Dedication

To the many students I have taught—all 3,706 of you. Each of you has helped me to grow and become a better teacher, and to my parents who were always there to encourage and support me in whatever I chose to do.

Contents

Acknowledgements

Not long ago, I overheard a conversation in which someone asked a young twenty something woman, "What do you do for a living?" Her response was, "Oh, I'm **just** a teacher." Although I was several feet away, sitting at another table in the restaurant, and obviously not a part of this conversation, I had to clench the table to keep myself from spinning around in my chair and saying, "Excuse me, but did I just hear you say **just** a teacher? What do you mean when you say **just** a teacher?"

For the past 28 years I have been a teacher. There's never been any "just" about it. Whether during my eighteen year tenure as an elementary classroom teacher or my nearly ten years as a college professor preparing future and practicing teachers, I see (and have always seen) my career choice as one of extreme importance and value.

At the time of this writing, I have worked with a total of 3,706 students (keeping track is just one of my unusual and curious behaviors). Some of them were children who are now adults raising children of their own, some of them were pre-service teachers who now write to me from their own classrooms across the United States, and some of them experienced practicing teachers who work with children 180 days each year. This book is dedicated to each of "my students." Over the years, we have shared many ideas, had meaningful discussions together, and enjoyed many pieces of literature. These former students with whom I spent many hours taught me as I taught them. Their questions challenged and broadened my thinking. Good literature brought us together and allowed us to learn from each other.

This book is also dedicated to the many teachers with whom I have worked over these 28 years. They have kindly welcomed me into their classrooms to talk and observe. They shared their ideas and their students as we introduced new books and tested new ideas. They allowed me to "pick" their brains and they shared wonderful insights into using literature with children. They were more than "just" teachers, and many of them have become my friends and colleagues. Their voices are heard throughout this book.

Most importantly, I am thankful to the special people in my life who supported me in this enormous effort. Sonja Gjurich and Shirelle Briscoe, my graduate assistants, who spent many hours proofreading to guard against my words sounding good only "in my own head." They helped me strive for clarity for all readers. Thank you.

Nedra Nastase, my friend and colleague, who gently pushed and continually encouraged me when I got tired and wanted to stop to do just about anything else! She knew how to remind me of the obstacles I had overcome and the progress I had made even when there were big mountains yet to climb. She is always one of my loudest and most appreciated "cheerleaders," and I am thankful to have her as both a friend and colleague.

My parents, Richard and Agnes Nypaver, who although they have never quite understood the long hours that a project such as this takes and how projects such as this can "take charge of one's life," they have always supported me in the most loving and understanding way. For all the visits I had to postpone and dinners I had to skip, I am now ready to make up for each of them. I give both of them a resounding "thank you" for the many years of support and encouragement and a tremendous debt of gratitude for believing in me.

Most of all, I am thankful to my husband, Greg, who so often waited patiently and who put up with a wife who was always working, feeling stressed, and, yes, sometimes cranky! Without his love, confidence, and understanding I would never have been able to do this. We can now look back as we smile, remember, and reclaim our weekends together.

Preface

I believe that a book should fit the audience. This book is written for a very important audience—classroom teachers working in kindergarten through grade four. You are a select group for a number of reasons; but, perhaps most importantly, I am writing this book for you because you have numerous opportunities to provide the early and positive experiences with literature that may affect children forever. You may not recognize it, but you and the books you use can change lives.

As I talk with practicing teachers, I have discovered that teachers have a number of questions when it comes to using literature in their classrooms. Betty, a third grade teacher in a rural school said, "I want to use books more, but as a busy teacher, I have no way to learn about what new books are out there. Consequently, I keep using the same old books year after year." Pat, a first grade teacher reports, "My district uses a basal reading series so what's a teacher to do? How can I move more toward literature when my district is not moving with me?" And Frank, a fourth grade teacher of over thirty years asked, "I think what really matters is that these kids can read. How are stories going to help that happen? That's why we have skills taught by the teacher and workbooks to practice those skills. What role can children's books really play?"

Over the years, these questions and others have been discussed around lunch tables in faculty lounges. They have perplexed pre-service teachers attempting to learn the "ways of schools and teaching" and puzzled practicing teachers who grapple with similar issues every day. Questions are sometimes boldly called out from audiences or more shyly asked during breaks when I do workshops and conference presentations. It is often difficult to give teachers satisfying answers to questions related to the use of literature in the classroom.

Although I don't profess to having all the answers, this book is an attempt to share many of my own personal experiences as a classroom teacher who always wanted to use literature more, but, at first, didn't know exactly how. It's a journey I'm anxious to share—a journey that can hopefully point out some of the values of using literature and encourage teachers to give it a chance in their classrooms. Most importantly, I hope that by offering teachers some information about many of the newest children's books as well as over 125 kid-tested and teacher approved ways to extend these stories into other areas of the curriculum, I can also answer the question one discouraged teacher recently asked, "So, I've read the book, now what do I do?"

I hope that teachers will see this book as a resource that they can refer to repeatedly rather than a one time read. I see it as a "jump start" for some teachers who are a little hesitant and uncertain. My hope is that after trying literature in some way in your classroom, whether you merely dangle your toes in the baby pool or plunge in off the high dive, you will meet with some level of success and have the desire and confidence to continue to use literature. My goal is that you will feel comfortable selecting books and planning activities that best meet the needs of your own students. I hope that this book will encourage, guide, and empower you toward the successful use of literature in your own classroom.

This book is divided into six chapters. Although I realize that teachers are always looking for ideas and activities, I felt it necessary to offer you more than that. I hope you will begin by reading the first five chapters to gain some insights that will help shape the way you use literature. You may have had few opportunities to share books with children, or, conversely, you may have had a great deal of experience with using literature. Whatever your background and personal experience, I hope this book will 1) enable you to enhance your professional judgement about using literature in your classroom; 2) guide you toward getting your children "hooked on books;" 3) aid you in designing opportunities for your children to respond to literature; and 4) suggest ways of making literature an even more valuable classroom resource. Most importantly, it is my hope that readers of *Using Literature in Your K–4 Classroom: Practical Ideas for Teachers* will develop a greater appreciation and renewed interest in using quality literature with the children they meet.

Barbara Nypaver Kupetz

Part 1

Understanding the Value
and Power of Literature

Part 1 sets the stage for using literature with children. As teachers, we will be more interested in and able to use literature effectively if we better understand the many benefits literature offers children. Chapter 1, "Why Should I Use Literature in My Classroom?" describes the numerous values and benefits of using quality literature selections with children. It helps explain why literature would be an important part of every classroom. Through many examples from actual classrooms and teacher vignettes, this chapter characterizes how literature is a powerful force in the lives of all of us and indeed touches children in important ways.

Chapter 2, "A Response-Centered, Literature-Rich Classroom" explores what is meant by the frequently used term, "response-centered" and helps those who work with children to understand how critical active involvement with literature is. It will help teachers consider what they are currently doing and compare it to the more child-centered and authentic use of literature this book supports. Together these two chapters provide a strong foundation for the remainder of this book.

1

Why Should I Use
Literature in My Classroom?

Almost as if it were magic, or as if light poured into her brain, the words and sentences started to take shape on the page as they never had before. "She . . . marched . . . them . . . off . . . to . . ."
Slowly, she read a sentence. Then another, and another. And finally she'd read a paragraph. And she understood the whole thing.
Patricia Polacco, 1998

This excerpt from Patricia Polacco's touching tribute to teachers highlights the powerful role each of us plays in the lives of the children we teach. We touch children every day; sometimes our influence is a very positive one and remembered by that particular student for a lifetime. Unfortunately, not every memory is a happy one and some of us hold in our heads memories of more unpleasant recollections that have lingered on into adulthood. A teacher's influence can be felt for a lifetime.

A Personal Story

Many of you who read this book will attest to being a product of an excellent teacher preparation program. I, too, believe that my undergraduate teaching gave me a strong foundation for my work in elementary classrooms. I also think that we will all admit there was and continues to be a great deal to be learned from our experiences as a teacher. Many of the important lessons we learn cannot be found within the pages of a book. It is a combination of our strong educational underpinnings and our daily experiential education that continue to make us better teachers. The ability to learn new things and to be a better teacher never ends.

Most likely you were taught to use a basal reading series to teach reading. Basal readers have come a long way over the years and today many schools continue to use them in the teaching of reading. I, too, used basals in my classroom teaching experiences; and I continue to use them as I show future teachers the options we have in designing a reading program. So, as I tell my students in the literacy classes I teach, "Kupetz is not saying throw out the basal!" What I am suggesting is that while I use the basal in my teaching, I have always had a strong interest in the integration of literature in my reading instruction.

I love children's books as many of you do. I have both pleasant and unpleasant memories of my childhood reading experiences that continue to play again in my mind. I remember being in the lowest reading group in second grade. The name of our group was the Canaries and we read with much more difficulty than the other more capable readers in the groups known as the Cardinals and Blue Jays. I can recall the humiliation of having to read aloud in front of my peers, displaying my many audible mistakes at which some of them giggled and others hurtfully teased. I can remember the many errors in my workbook, which were highlighted by the teacher's red pen, and how the workbook pages were sent home for my parents to see. Reading was not a happy time for me as a young student and, as I struggled, I found no enjoyment in books at all.

When third grade began, I met a person who changed my life, and that introduction nurtured a relationship with a teacher who loved books. For Sister Canice, books were a passion. Every day, she carried the one she was currently reading into the classroom and placed it on the corner of her desk—that was the special spot reserved for her book. I can still close my eyes and clearly see the old and especially worn leather marker that jutted out from the pages of her book. We could all tell that each book was special to her.

But, more important than the books she read herself were the books she read to us. Each day, after we returned from the playground following lunch, she read aloud to us. It was when I heard her read that I knew this was something I wanted to be able to do. Her words were so powerful. It seemed not to matter what she read, but how she read. With such fluency and expression, she took us all on a journey to new places, introduced us to characters we would never have known, and taught us about ways of living so different from what we knew in a small, western Pennsylvania coal mining town.

Sister Canice was one of the most powerful role models I have encountered and her enthusiasm for literature was simply contagious. Although I could not read well and certainly didn't possess the ability to demonstrate fluency and expression as I read aloud, I knew this was what I aspired to do—read books and read them well. That year I read (as labored as it was) many books aloud to my mother and enjoyed her reading to me. I became interested in the Nancy Drew series and that summer I struggled through three of them from start to finish. What an accomplishment for this challenged reader! I can remember keeping a chart to show my slow, but steady progress.

Through fourth and fifth grades, I continued to work hard and read and read and read. It would be an untruth to say something miraculous happened and suddenly I could read! That did not happen. But it is true to say that when one teacher shared with me wonderful books and her enthusiasm for books and reading, I realized I wanted to be able to enjoy books as she did and I worked and worked to become a better reader. I more willingly accepted the support of other adults who knew of my dream and desire to become what I called a "real reader."

By the end of elementary school, I was a "real reader" (I suppose my teachers would have termed it "average to above average"). Even more significant was my appetite for reading. I still saw Sister Canice carrying her book with her when I passed her in the halls of the school, but now something was different—I, too, carried a book and I absolutely loved all that books had to offer.

Maybe it was because of how hard I had to work to make books a part of my life that I always held a special place in my heart and my classroom for books. I guess I'll never really know why it happened, but when I began teaching I was not satisfied with simply using the basal reader. Maybe it was because I knew of so many wonderful stories I felt my students might not come to know unless someone shared them. Maybe it was because reading literature had opened so many doors for me and had introduced me to people, places, and information I would not have otherwise come to know. Whatever the reason, I always found a way to bring children's literature to my students. I loved children's books and wanted to share them with my children in every way I could.

I did use the basal reader because that was required by the school district in which I taught, but I also read aloud to my children in every grade I taught and I did it every day (I even read daily to my college students). After a few weeks of reading aloud, the students questioned me if I forgot or found it had to be skipped. "Where is our story?" they'd ask. I knew these children loved books as much as I did. I thought, "Wouldn't this be a wonderful way to get them excited about reading?" I thought about it a lot.

When my teaching took me to another grade in another school, I gave considerable thought to finding ways to integrate children's books into my classroom in a variety of ways, particularity into my reading program. What was to follow was a series of years where I tried a variety of ways to refine and improve my reading program and my teaching. I felt very strongly about being able to offer my students two things.

First, the skills they needed to successfully learn and improve their reading; knowing how to read could not be underestimated. And second, to be exposed to the many wonderful children's books in such ways that it would not only support their learning, but get them as excited as I was about books. This has never stopped being my passion.

I believe from my own experiences as a child, as well as what I have seen in my own students, that children learn through literature in many different ways. I never stopped teaching my children to read, but I did teach them with fewer dittos (that word alone dates me doesn't it?) and black line masters and more authentic child-centered activities where they could be actively involved. There was less reliance on the basal reader and less of what I began to call "drill 'em, skill 'em, kill 'em" activities. It has been for my students and me a comfortable blend and integration of a reading series and literature.

The books we bring to children offer yet another way to "touch" them through engaging stories, life-like characters, and wonderfully descriptive settings. These stories might help a child see his own experiences with a new baby mirrored in *Julius, the Baby of the World* (Henkes, 1990); identify with the feelings of Max, who after being scolded, takes off in his imagination to *Where the Wild Things Are* (Sendak,1963). Older children can experience the loneliness and anxiety of an African American girl who must face an all-white environment when her family moves to the suburbs in Pinkney's *Hold Fast to Your Dreams* (1995); the emotional growth and coming to terms with oneself that Heather "lives" in Conrad's (1985) *Staying Nine*; or the toughness and resiliency of a foster child in Katherine Paterson's *The Great Gilly Hopkins* (1978). Because of the multitude of benefits inherent in using literature with children and the important role it plays in their language, cognitive, social, and personality development, it seems that almost all teachers would welcome it into their classroom. Yet, some still have questions about the need to make it an integral part of the curriculum. How do you feel?

Another Teacher's Thoughts

I think a good story is great, but what about learning to read? Isn't that more important? A book is something I fit in whenever we have a few free minutes—after lunch or before dismissal. It isn't something I have time to do every day. Anyone can read children a book. I am here to teach them.

Joanne, third grade teacher

How do you feel after reading Joanne's comments about sharing books with children? Do you agree? Disagree? Joanne is not alone. There are teachers who view using literature with children as "an extra"—something that we fit in when we can, but so often we can't. Reading books is often what gets "left out."

From Joanne's comments, we can make several assumptions. First, we might speculate that Joanne does not really enjoy reading herself. Perhaps she has not had positive and pleasurable experiences with books and they are not placed as high on her list of priorities as some other things. Secondly, we might assume that Joanne has not recently had a course in children's literature or hasn't attended any professional development workshops or seminars regarding books and reading. Perhaps she does not have the "tools" or confidence to successfully use literature with children. Maybe she does not see literature as a good use of her time or that of the children in her classroom. Could it be that Joanne simply does not recognize all that literature could offer her students?

Joanne is representative of a number of teachers who hold a common misconception that children's literature encompasses darling books for children that are not really worthy of serious educational consideration. These teachers might see the reading level and content as simple and the pictures as cute and attention getting. To them, the appeal and value of children's literature is not considered important, although today's children's literature is the subject of research, social controversy, and literary and artistic criticism. In many classrooms, it is becoming a more important part of school curricula than ever before.

Children's literature has always been a meaningful part of children's lives. Not only is it worthy of being shared by adults but good books serve children in some very specific and important ways (see figure 1.1). Good children's books can evoke strong feelings and come to represent childhood emotions, much as a favorite stuffed animal or security blanket. The right story can help children better understand themselves and others through the characters they meet and the experiences they share. Many selections of children's literature can cultivate a child's capacity for empathy and compassion, educate the imagination, and invite children to enjoy and play with language. Sharing books with children helps them develop a visual and artistic sense, an appreciation and awareness all their own. Children's literature is a means of keeping alive the literary heritage of days gone by. A well-crafted story can nurture one's understanding of and appreciation for diversity of all kinds. Good books give the reader new information through differing perspectives and can provide vicarious experiences unlike any other opportunities the reader may have. Perhaps most importantly good children's books offer enjoyment and pleasure. This is where we can start.

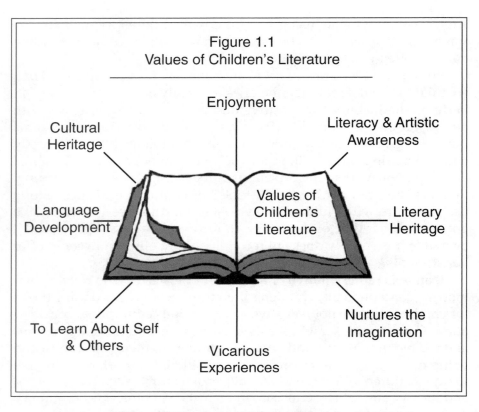

Figure 1.1
Values of Children's Literature

Enjoyment

Cultural Heritage

Literacy & Artistic Awareness

Language Development

Values of Children's Literature

Literary Heritage

To Learn About Self & Others

Vicarious Experiences

Nurtures the Imagination

Benefits of Learning Through Literature

Pleasurable Experiences

> Tikki tikki tembo-no sa rembo-chari bari ruchi-pip peri pembo ran as fast as his little legs could carry him to his mother and said, "Most Honorable Mother, Chang has fallen into the well!" (Mosel, 1968, p. 15)

> Wilbur never forgot Charlotte. Although he loved her children and grandchildren dearly, none of the new spiders ever quite took her place in his heart. She was in a class by herself. It is not often that someone comes along who is a true friend and a good writer. Charlotte was both. (White, 1952, p. 184)

Can you easily remember and identify these excerpts from popular children's books? Do they bring a smile to your face as you remember the pleasurable experiences they offered you? For each of us, special titles or excerpts help us remember that books have brought us delight, entertainment, and pleasure. Whether the words and pictures provide totally new insights or offer quite familiar experiences, they can be fun and offer great satisfaction to the reader. Pleasure persuades and encourages the child to first have interest in and look more closely at the book, then to read it, talk about it, and next to remember it as a personal favorite. Children must enjoy the book for it to win the ever raging battle between books and the color and animation of today's toys, television, and computers. Therefore, getting pleasure from a good book is a prerequisite for developing an appreciation for books and continuing to seek them out.

Whether it is the rhythm the reader encounters in *Five Little Monkeys* (Christelow, 1990); the silly antics of that zany housekeeper in *Amelia Bedelia* (Parish, 1992); the adventures of Max as he travels in out of days and weeks in *Where the Wild Things Are* (Sendak, 1963); the sadness we feel because of the loss of a real friend in *Charlotte's Web* (White, 1952); the way in which one's imagination is sparked by *James and the Giant Peach* (Dahl, 1961); or those "morphing" children in the *Animorph* series by K. A. Applegate, it is clear that books have so much enjoyment to offer every reader regardless of interests or reading ability.

As children examine pictures, imagine knowing and befriending new characters, think of life in a new and different place, or experience some amazing adventures unlike anything they could ever experience in their own lives, they develop an appreciation for literature and they are touched by the enjoyment a good book can offer. As teachers, our goal should be to develop life-long readers. Our task goes beyond simply teaching children to read.

The very best gift we could give our students is a love of and enthusiasm for books which they can carry with them forever. As adults, we can look back on the past and probably remember our teachers and parents speaking of the importance of reading. They reminded us often. Many of us can recall the catchy bookmarks with memorable slogans like "Books can take you anywhere" and "Dive into a good book!" As adults, we recognize how true these words are. Most teachers would no doubt agree with Jim Trelease, a long time advocate of using literature with children, when at a speaking engagement he said, "The desire to read is not born in a child—it is planted. The only rational way of educating is by example. Show them how—read aloud!" Indeed, literacy is so much more than merely the recitation of words and mastery of skills.

Jalongo (1988) describes literacy operating on the "iceberg principle." The knowledge of taught reading skills makes up only the tip of the iceberg, yet it is what we can most easily see above the surface of the water. But there, below the surface, is the bigger part of the iceberg—the substantial and crucially important *feelings* about reading. As teachers who undoubtedly care about children being able to read, we need to look closely and consider that it is not only important to help children develop into individuals who can read but also those who choose to read. Well developed reading skills only serve us well if we use them. Would we be satisfied with producing "skill strong" children who know how to read but choose not to read? I hope not.

Yes, we should care that children have basic reading skills and can read, but equally important is our need to care that children want to read. Sharing good literature with children, modeling enthusiasm for books, and providing opportunities for responding to books in active and personal ways are all excellent means to get children "hooked on books" like no basal reading series alone can. Judith O'Malley, editor of *Books Links,* wrote about reading and the use of trade books in a 1997 editorial. Her words remind us of our role as teachers and the power of using trade books with children. O'Malley says,

> When we use trade books in the curriculum, our hope is to
> spark the flame of curiosity and interest with a gripping story,
> then have a stack of firewood handy in the form of wonderful
> books that fan the flame to extend the experience of learning
> and reading. But the ultimate goal is to equip children to light
> their own matches of curiosity, of discovery, and gather the
> wood of additional resources themselves. (p. 5)

I believe teachers using literature, shared with passion, enjoyment and desire, can do just that.

Today, there are many excellent books for children, and it is estimated that several thousand more are published each year. With such an array of books, there must be something to meet the needs and interests of everyone! There are books that can offer even the toughest critic a fun and pleasurable experience.

Children need the encouragement, modeling, and assistance of a teacher who loves books, too. Each of us plays a critical role in getting children "hooked on books." Many years ago, a college professor told me something that I have always remembered and frequently pass on to others because I believe it to be so true. She said, "Excitement about and enthusiasm for books cannot be taught, but it can be caught." Books should be read for many reasons, but especially for the fun and pleasure they offer. Get your students excited about books through the example you demonstrate in your classroom.

Developing Literary and Artistic Awareness

If your local bookstore gave you a gift certificate valued at $100.00 and allowed you to spend it on any books you'd like, what would you select? Some would immediately go to the Stephen King section loving a good and often gruesome scare, others a juicy romance novel, some the travel section, and yet others directly to the cookbooks, or sports writers. Many would prefer biographies, some would seek out books by a favorite political satirist, and yet others would select books with the photographs of a particular photojournalist they have come to enjoy. Why? Because each of us has developed some level of both literary and artistic awareness. Simply stated, we know what we like and seek that when selecting books. Whether our choices are based on the topic or writing style, the genre or the illustrations, we know how we want to spend our $100.00!

Each of us, through our experiences with books and life, have decided what we enjoy most—it is our literary awareness. This awareness changes over time and today is certainly not what it was when we were children. We use our life experiences, our interests, and what we have come to know about the writing of certain authors to shape the choices we make. But what about children? Do they have literary and artistic awareness? Let's look at some examples.

Peter is three. His mother reports that he brings the same book to her again, and again, and again, although he has many from which to select. His mother grimaces as she reveals that she has memorized the book and can hardly bear to read it one more time! But she does and Peter giggles with delight with each reading.

Jennifer is eight and in third grade. Her teacher notices that each week she returns her library book only to ask for another by the same writer/illustrator, Tomie dePaola. She requests his books each week saying, "I like his pictures the very best."

Tayesha, a second grader, asked the librarian at her school, "Do you have any more books by Peggy Rathman? That Officer Buckle story was so good. I think she writes really funny stories."

Jake, a fourth grader who struggles with reading, has become interested in a biography series which offers in-depth profiles of names in the entertainment and arts, science, social studies, and sports world. These books have recently grabbed the attention of Jake and he proudly tells his reading teacher, "I have already read four of them, Mrs. Bickman. I read about Andre Agassi, Wayne Gretzky, Cal Ripken, Jr., and my favorite was Michael Jordan. I'm keeping a list to see if I can read the 26 other biographies about famous men in baseball, football, hockey, and basketball 'cause those are the sports I like best."

Peter, Tayesha, Jennifer, and Jake have identified books that appeal to them and pique their interests in some particular way. These authors and illustrators, the styles of their books, and the genres help form their literary and artistic awareness. When does it happen that we know what we like? For those children who have many opportunities to experience books, it can happen quite early. For those who have limited experiences with books, it becomes almost impossible to know what you'd like to read if you haven't "tasted the flavors" and experienced the variety of books offered.

Perhaps the analogy to food is appropriate here. When adults expose children to many different kinds of foods, they come to know the taste of each and are better equipped to make knowledgeable decisions about which foods they'd like to try again. For these children, a list of favorite foods may include a large number of different things. But those who are exposed to limited kinds of food have so little from which to choose that their list of favorites may be very short. As teachers, parents, and adults who work with children, we owe it to our young charges to open up the world of possibilities when it comes to books. Exposure to a variety of types of literature helps the reader/listener develop a literary awareness—knowing what you like. Opening the world of literature to children allows them to develop into discriminating readers who have discovered their personal favorites. Only then can children develop a literary and artistic awareness based on the wide variety of "flavors" available through the world of books.

Our Literary Heritage

Books do not simply help us develop our own personal literary and artistic awareness, they also allow us to keep alive our literary heritage. Throughout the history of children's literature we have had many books which have delighted audiences. These stories have survived the test of time because of their quality and enduring entertainment. Using literature with children allows us to introduce them to these classic selections. Even today, we can enjoy the stories of the March family as told by Louisa May Alcott and the fairy tales of Charles Perrault. We can share the excitement of the adventures of Robinson Crusoe or Jonathan Swift's 1726 tales of Gulliver. We can still delight in Beatrix Potter's turn of the century tales of Peter Rabbit. We can appreciate life in the south through the humorous yet very revealing tales of Uncle Remus by Joel Chandler Harris (1881), even though they are more than one hundred years old. Readers can learn of family life of the past as they read *The Moffats* (Estes, 1941) or of the more contemporary families we meet in Beverly Cleary's Ramona or Danzinger's Amber Brown series. One of the freshest looks at family life can be found in David Adler's *The Many Troubles of Andy Russell* (1998).

Today, in addition to students creating their own list of favorites which they may pass on to their children as their personal literary and artistic heritage, they can enjoy those many classic favorites their parents, grandparents, and teachers have savored in their youth and which today comprise a literary heritage to which we connect and remember. Books such as *Make Way for Ducklings* (McCloskey, 1941), *Curious George* (Rey, 1941), *Where the Wild Things Are* (Sendak, 1963), and *The Mouse and the Motorcycle* (Cleary, 1965) constitute a literary heritage that lives on. Being familiar with a variety of genre of literature, knowing what we enjoy reading, and being able to identify and take with us into adolescence and adulthood our own literary heritage are other important values of using literature with children.

Nurturing the Imagination

In an age when television and computer technology make details so explicit through wonderful color and catchy animation, the competition between books and technology is fierce. Today we find that children use their imaginations less than in the past. In some ways, our advanced technology reduces a need for imagination, but books can support and facilitate the creative spirit. This is not to say that children should stop viewing television or select to abandon technology only to read books. That would not be realistic. However, it is realistic to hope that teachers will elect to use books in their classrooms that will help the reader/listener "see" with an "inner eye" and build pictures and ideas not represented on a colorful electronic screen.

Children's literature offers many opportunities to imagine. For instance, *Sarah Plain and Tall* (MacLachlan, 1985), *Dandelions* (Bunting, 1995), or *Mississippi Mud: Three Prairie Journals* (Turner, 1997) all provide opportunities to imagine life in a different time. For a child living in a rural community, a very different picture is painted and a new experience lived vicariously when the reader enjoys Faith Ringold's *Tar Beach* (1991). As Nikke, a curious six year old, wondered aloud while her teacher shared the Ringold's book, "Where do the boys and girls play there?"

John Scieszka's *Your Mother Was a Neanderthal* (1993) allows the reader to take part in a journey back in time to the days of the wooly, mammoth, and saber toothed tiger. Each individual's ability to imagine can be sparked through the imagery, characters, and setting of a good book.

Vicarious Experiences

I can still remember the first time I visited the beach when I was a child of about ten. It was an experience filled with so many emotions— excitement and fear, surprise and disappointment, questions and answers. I can remember asking what it would be like and my mother (the water lover in the family) trying to describe all the nuances of the sand and surf to this inquisitive young child. Her words helped to paint a picture for me. In my mind's eye, I tried to see what I would soon experience.

In preparation for my trip, I remembered going to the library and finding a book about seashells. I made a list of all the prettiest or most unusual shells because it was my plan to find these when I traveled to the beach. For all of us who have been to the beach this approach to shell collecting seems a bit ridiculous, but to a 10-year old with no prior "beach experiences," it seemed the appropriate thing to do. That book and my mother's stories were all I had to create a bridge between the known and the unknown. They provided a vicarious experience for me as a young reader until I could touch the shells, splash in the waves, feel the sand between my toes, hear the seagulls calling, and experience all of the other indigenous features of the beach by actually being there.

Books provide children with vicarious experiences whether it's one of being a migrant worker on a farm, living as a child during the Holocaust, or spending a week at the ocean. The expression we often see on reading posters, "Books can take you anywhere" is certainly true. Through the pages of a book, we can visit real worlds of long ago or futuristic worlds of tomorrow. Good writing can transport us.

Learning About Ourselves and Others

Good literature reflects life. Through it we see our world—the good and the bad, the familiar and the unfamiliar. We see ourselves and others within the pages of a book. In the book, *For Love of Reading: A Parent's Guide for Encouraging Young Readers from Infancy Through Age 5*, Rudman and Pearce (1988) remind us of this when they say, "Books can serve as mirrors for children . . . and windows on our world" (p. 159). The analogy of books to mirrors and windows aptly describes how the printed word cannot only allow readers to peer into a world unlike their own, but can also allow readers to see reflections of their own lives. This analogy also suggests the individuality of a reader's response—a book which may serve as a mirror for one child as it reflects characters or experiences similar to her own life, may create very different connections for another reader. Literature strongly supports the notion of individuality and how singularly we appreciate and understand books.

For me, Cynthia Rylant's book, *Missing May* (1992) is truly a mirror. When Summer lost her dear Aunt May with whom she lived, I felt her sorrow, pain, and loneliness. I immediately made connections to the difficult times I faced with the loss of my grandmother many years ago. I empathized with Summer and Uncle Ob and knew that the strength to carry them forward would come in time.

Conversely, as I read Eve Bunting's (1991) *Fly Away Home*, I felt something very different. This book gave me the opportunity to look into a world quite unlike my own. I could not relate to this book in the same kind of personal way, but it served as a "window" into the world of homelessness, which raised my level of awareness and triggered empathy and compassion in a different, yet heart-felt way. It caused me to pause a moment and consider the struggles and the needs of those who face the daily battles of homelessness.

Take a minute to consider the books you have recently read. Think of one which was a mirror for you—a book in which you could see examples of familiar people or experiences. And a window? What book broadened your world in some way because it offered you a glimpse at a world outside your own experiences?

Are books powerful influences in the lives of children? Can they at times provide comfort, solutions to problems, a bridge from one's small and familiar world to one which is new and different? The answer is "yes." Books can do this and so much more.

Books can touch us in special and very important ways. The road of emotional growth can be a very bumpy one, but a natural part of the process we call "growing up." Literature can make a positive contribution to our emotional growth. As children read or listen to quality children's literature, they begin to recognize that all of us experience problems, and often that we may share similar problems not only with book characters but with our peers. Books can offer options for dealing with such problems as the reader/listener learns how characters effectively deal with their given situations.

Today, there are many books offering this kind of inner picture of ourselves and empathy for others. Some of the popular series with which children have made real life connections include Lois Lowry's Anastasia Krupnik series, Ann Cameron's Julian stories, and Louis Sacher's tales of the Wayside School. These books are enjoyed by many third and fourth graders who see themselves and their everyday experiences within these pages. Also, Patricia Reilly Giff's *Adventures of the Kids of the Polk Street School* and the *Henry and Mudge* series by Cynthia Rylant offer the same kinds of connections for six to nine year olds who are just beginning to be a part of school groups and have their own set of ups and downs. These books and many others help readers of all ages learn more about themselves and others.

Look at the books in your classroom library. How many can you find that focus on the common everyday experiences of the children you teach? Maybe you'll find *Franklin in the Dark* (Bourgeois, 1986), a book about accepting and meeting our fears; *Ira Sleeps Over* (Waber, 1973), a tale of the apprehensions that might be felt at the time of that first sleepover; *Leo the Late Bloomer* (Kraus, 1971), a story that indicates to children (and their parents) that we all come to achieve certain things in our own good time; *Meet Calliope Day* (Haddad, 1998), the humorous escapades about a feisty "Ramona-gets-into-trouble" type child; *Dear Mr. Henshaw* (Cleary, 1983) the tale of a boy caught in the middle of a family divorce; and *Tight Times* (Hazen, 1983) a story that, at first, seems to portray a somewhat sad picture of a family caught in the throws of unemployment, but one that portrays a family that sees the optimism that is present even in the most bleak situations. No doubt, you will find a number of books that reflect the concerns and issues that are important in the lives of the children you teach.

From these books, children can learn to recognize that they are not alone in the issues that affect their lives and to gain new perspectives on dealing with their situations. They may also learn to better appreciate and understand these experiences as they take on the perspectives others. Whether the books children read present themselves as a "mirror" or a "window," each book has its own way of teaching children about themselves and others.

Language Development

Jonathan, who was five, took the book *The Gingerbread Man* (Kimmel, 1993) from the hands of his three-year-old sister and said, "Here, let me read it to you." Jonathan's father was not surprised by this even though Jonathan could not "read" as some more strictly define reading. What Jonathan did do was "read" his sister the story he had heard many times before in his own special way. According to Ken Goodman's (1986) definition of reading, Jonathan did read for he was a part of "a process in which a person reconstructs a message graphically encoded by a writer" (p. 75). He understood enough about language and the structure of stories to retell his story using the pictures for prompts.

Jonathan began with "Once upon a time . . ." and as he went on, it was clear to the observer that he was a seasoned book lover! He used good expression and changed his voice as he retold the story in his own words. You could feel the enthusiasm in his voice as he chanted, "Run, run as fast as you can. You can't catch me I'm the gingerbread man." He encouraged his young sibling to notice certain things in the picture with remarks like, "See there goes the gingerbread man again," as he pointed to the picture. Once, he even asked his sister to join in on the repetitive lines of the story. "Come on Taylor, say it with me, 'Run, run as fast as you can. You can't catch me I'm the gingerbread man.'" Taylor repeated "gingerbread man" and pointed to the picture with a wide, ear-to-ear smile.

Although there are different views on how children develop language including the behaviorist, maturational, cognitive-developmental, and psycholinguistic (Dale, 1976; Loban, 1976), we can all agree that providing a rich language environment for children has a profound influence on language development. One way to do this is through the sharing of literature.

Anyone who has been around young children recognizes the potential for remarkable language development during the first few years of life. First they (to the delight of everyone) make early babbling vocalizations. Adults gather around encouraging more. Language development proceeds to the use of a few sounds that may represent words ("buh-bah" for bottle) and the initial utterances of nouns such as "cookie" or "dada." Soon, children begin to add verbs to their speech ("eat cookie" and "dada run") and later acquire adjectives ("good cookie"). These examples of prelinguistic and telegraphic speech are just the beginning of many years of language development and refinement. Time passes and because children are surrounded with models of language, their skills are honed with the addition of adverbs and more nouns and adjectives. Soon young children will use language to question, and they will eventually begin to use grammatically correct sentences. They have learned to effectively master words and use the communicative process. They themselves have become communicators.

Throughout these years of developing language skills, parents, caregivers, and teachers have opportunities as well as the obligation to provide a good model for language use and encouragement for future development. Through simple and ongoing conversations with adults, children have opportunities to "use" language and practice their skills. They see models of how language works. Such models are also available through the books we share with children.

For a very young child just learning to "make" words and language, a child for whom English is a second language, or a child enthralled with the rhythm and cadence of language, the sometimes repetitive language of books can be delightful. In Don and Audrey Wood's (1984) *The Napping House,* the repetitive phrase "where everyone is sleeping" needs only to be read a few times before all young children are ready to join in the refrain. Older children are intrigued by the ingenious uses of language in stories such as Norton Jester's (1961) *The Phantom Tollbooth,* Ellen Raskin's *The Westing Game* (1978), Pilkey's (1994) *Dog Breath,* or Dahl's (1982) *BFG* . Language can be great as the words in a book paint breathtaking images or offer a child ways to explore whole new areas of interest.

For Matt, the language of books helped him cultivate his knowledge and "talk the talk" of biking as he began saving up his allowance to buy a new bike. He searched the library at school as well as the public library for books about bikes and bicycling. He became quite the "bike expert," and his favorite bike book was Hautzig's (1996) *Pedal Power:*

How a Mountain Bike is Made. He began to use some of his newly acquired, specialized vocabulary in conversations with family and friends. This included words like "sprockets," "pneumatic tires," "cable housing," and "forks." Matt's developing language and the resulting expanded vocabulary was an outgrowth of being highly motivated about a particular topic and the language of the books he devoured. As we can see in Matt's example, books offer children the tools to expand their speaking vocabularies.

Cultural Heritage and Literature

Geri, a seasoned teacher of 28 years recalls her childhood and the books and television that she experienced.

> When I was growing up and reading about Dick and Jane and later Nancy Drew, I saw no characters within the pages of the books I read who looked anything like my family. Almost every character was white, and I wasn't white! Almost every character seemed to be middle class and although we had lots of love, we didn't have any money. My family portrait seemed so different from the families in the books I read. Even the popular television culture of the day showed a different kind of family. I can still remember *Leave It to Beaver.* It showed Mr. Cleaver bursting into the family home after a day at the office calling, "Hello Marge, I'm home!" The mother ran from the kitchen to greet him. She had on a perfectly clean, pressed dress and didn't have a hair out of place! That wasn't the way it looked at my house around five o'clock! The television shows and the books that were available to me didn't resemble my family or my life in the least!

Most children's books written in the decades before the 1970s introduced characters who were white and middle class. Nancy Larrick, in her revealing 1965 article "The All-White World of Children's Books," addressed this serious issue of omission as she transported the reader into the world of an African American five-year-old who asked, "Why are they always white children?" Larrick summarized this literary deficiency when she stated, "Integration may be the law of the land, but most of the books children see are all white" (p. 63).

Throughout the late 60s and early 70s, as a result of our nations' increasingly pluralistic society as well as the social consciousness aroused by the Civil Rights Movement, there was an increasing consumer demand for books representing diversity. But what do we mean when we refer to books representing "diversity"? Is it only those books which reflect racial minorities?

Although over the last two decades we have used the term "multicultural literature" to describe books with characters representing a variety of races, we now recognize diversity as encompassing much more than only race. A more contemporary description would include literature which shows a broad range of differences including, but not limited to, ethnicity, race, culture, linguistics, sexual orientation, disability, age, or gender roles (Bishop, 1997; Horning & Kruse, 1991; Ford, 1994). Today, literature plays an important role in helping children (and adults) understand and appreciate one's own cultural heritage as well as the cultural heritage and diversity of others. As we look around this world in which we live, we see diversity at every turn. Do the books we use in our classrooms reflect the many kinds of diversity?

Whether it is the black child in an urban school, the child raised in a home with less traditional gender roles, a child whose family configuration is not that of the once more common family unit of mother, father, and children, or a child with special needs—all readers deserve to see people like themselves within the pages of the books they read. As children see the similarities and differences (yes, there are both, although some adults believe it accurate to tell children "we are all the same"), they can better understand and appreciate these differences that do exist. The result is a more positive attitude, a reduction of biases, and greater respect for ourselves and others. Well selected books give children the ability to develop a worldview that not only celebrates their own uniqueness but also appreciates the uniqueness in others.

Books offer us points of comparison for our own lives. Geri again shares some of her memories as she was growing up.

> I was not like Jane as she appeared in my basal reader, nor was
> I like the other characters I read about. I was like someone I
> could not find. Unfortunately I thought I was so different that
> I was ashamed of my family's culture.

Today, books allow the reader/listener to recognize common bonds, similarities, and the universality of experiences that exist irrespective of one's race, culture, age, disability, language, family configuration, or ethnicity. As you read Mary Hoffman's book, *Amazing Grace* (1991) to your students, they don't just see a young black child who is told she can't be Peter Pan because of her gender and skin color. Instead, they meet a young girl who learns that no matter who you may be, hard work and determination are what helps us achieve our dreams. It is a universal message like this one that allows books to teach us so much.

Children need to make connections. Does the literature you select relate to the child who "lives" with the ups and downs of childhood such as making friends, being accepted by others, sibling rivalry, fitting into the school community, and the give and take of family life. These types of ever present issues can be explored as the reader meets characters like Alexander in *Alexander and the Terrible, Horrible, No Good, Very Bad Day* (Viorst, 1972), Julian and his brother in *The Stories Julian Tells* (Cameron, 1987), or Annie Bananie in *Annie Bananie Best Friends to the End* (Komaiko, 1997).

The themes in the books we read also reflect our life experiences. We read about compassion in *The Beast in Mrs. Rooney's Room* (Giff, 1985), independence in *Ira Sleeps Over* (Waber, 1972), pride and accomplishment in *Leo, the Late Bloomer* (Kraus, 1994), and true friendship in *Best Friends* (Kellogg, 1986). Literature shines on all of us with a bright light that crosses all cultures, races, genders, ages, and socioeconomic backgrounds. We all share so much and books can help show young readers the universality of our experiences.

Involving Children in Literature

Whether we are developing a literature program, supplementing an existing literature program, or simply sharing wonderful books with the children we teach, we should remember the dual roles of using literature: offering a child life-long enjoyment and developing understanding of the printed word. If you hope to develop this understanding, then it is necessary to give children many opportunities to read wonderful stories, hear others read stories and offer a good model of reading, share stories with each other, and discuss and respond to literature in a variety of ways. Although chapters 2–5 are specifically designed to discuss the "whys" and "hows" leading to this goal and chapter 6 actually provides a number of literature selections and activities, this section will briefly share ways to involve children to promote understanding.

Using literature supports the trend in educational reforms calling for children to think critically. In recent years, in order to improve critical thinking and problem solving skills, many schools have included critical thinking as a part of their long range strategic plans and have purchased expensive commercial programs that promise to improve such skills through workbooks and worksheets. Educators might find it less expensive and more enjoyable, for both teachers and students, to think of literature as a more natural and available way to reach the same goal. As we look at the operations of thinking including observing, comparing, classifying, organizing, summarizing, applying, criticizing, and questioning, we can see multiple ways in which using literature employs and enhances these skills.

Colorful picture books are an excellent way to develop observational skills in both younger and older children. Many of us will recall the *Where's Waldo* books popular in the 1980s. Children were intrigued with them and spent long periods of time using their observational skills trying to find Waldo. Today, there are many new books to stimulate and encourage the use of keen observational skills. One such book is *Look Once, Look Twice* (Marshall, 1995). This book provides the reader with the clue of an alphabet letter as well as a "peek" at a part of the picture as the reader observes, hypothesizes, and then makes an inference about the hidden picture to identify the letter.

Children find in Stephen Johnson's (1994) unique alphabet book, *Alphabet City*, and its wordless companion book, *City by Numbers* (1999), fascinating ways to look for the common letters and numbers in their everyday surroundings. Books such as these call upon the reader to use observational skills to recognize common objects in more unusual ways. Another such book, *Look-Alikes* (Steiner, 1998), invites readers to a land where the more you look the more you see! Here, the reader's eye sees a three-dimensional world created using everything from acorns to zippers. What fun to hone our observational skills in this way!

Literature selections offer many opportunities for children to make comparisons from the simplest one's in Tana Hoban's (1983) *Exactly the Opposite* to the character comparisons children will make as they compare and contrast themselves to the characters in the books they read. A book that seems to never lose kid appeal and offers a wonderful vehicle for children to talk comfortably is *Alexander and the Terrible, Horrible, No Good, Very Bad Day* (Viorst, 1972). All any teacher has to ask is, "Have you every had a terrible, horrible, no good, very bad day like Alexander? Let's look at the things that happened to him and think about those terrible, horrible, no good, very bad things that have happened to us" and the comparisons will naturally flow. One teacher followed that discussion with one about a wonderful, terrific, great, fabulous, awesome day the students might have had.

Teachers can also use a variety of differently illustrated versions of a story such as the many versions of the *Velveteen Rabbit* that Margery Williams first published in 1922, or any one of the classic selections of folklore including *The Little Red Hen* (Galdone, 1973), *Cinderella* (Perrault, 1954), or *The Breman Town Musicians* (Grimm & Grimm, 1992). Each has a number of different "tellings" and offer children many opportunities to sharpen their comparison skills by identifying the similarities and differences in text illustrations.

Also, remember to include some of the more contemporary fairy tale variants. What can you discover in terms of similarities and differences between *The Emperor's New Clothes* (Anderson, 1982) and the newer retelling with a twist titled *The Principal's New Clothes* (Calmenson,1989) or the modern variant of another favorite tale with a new rhyming "rap" twist, *Rapunzel: A Happenin Rap* (Vozar, 1998).

Another story reminiscent of an old and familiar favorite is *Fanny's Dream* (Buehner, 1996). Although not reflected in its title, this tale prompted a great deal of comparison in the conversations of a group of children enrolled in a Title I program. Shortly after the teacher began reading the story aloud, Clarissa's comment reflected that she was already making comparisons when she shouted out, "You know, this is kinda like Cinderella because she wants to go to the dance and so did Cinderella, but the fairy godmother isn't coming." As the teacher continued to read, other children called out similarities and differences. This teacher was excited about how well the children understood the idea of similarities and differences, and followed the story with additional discussion compairing these two stories with quite different titles. The Venn Diagram in Figure 1.2 shows some of their findings.

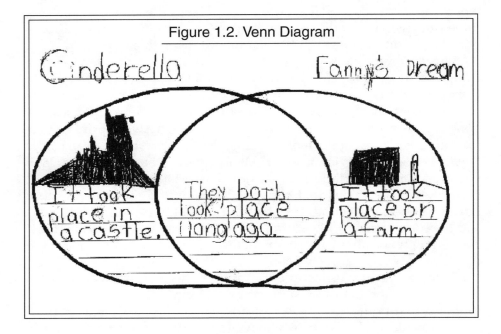

Figure 1.2. Venn Diagram

Many types of books can be used to develop and strengthen children's classifying skills. For example, children can begin to classify the books they enjoy as real or make believe, story animals as wild, farm, or pet animals. Also, objects from stories can be classified by attribute. An example would be the chairs, beds, and bowls of porridge in *The Three Bears* (Barton, 1991) as being the smallest, medium, and largest. Other ideas encouraging classification would include classification by color after reading Tana Hoban's *Colors Everywhere* (1995). What else can we find in our school or neighborhood that is each of these colors? Another excellent photo concept is Hoban's *Is it Larger? Is it Smaller?* (1985). These books as well as many others provide opportunities for young children to classify through the use of literature.

For the older student, *Safari* (Bateman, 1998) is a book with a format shaped by classification. Information about each African animal is categorized by habitat, enemies, preferred food, and other topics.

Hypothesizing

"Look at the cover of the story we are reading today. Look at the pictures carefully. What do you think today's story will be about?" This type of introduction to a read-aloud is often heard as teachers encourage even the youngest students to hypothesize or search for clues in pictures and text. Teachers often ask questions during the reading of a book that prompt children to consider "What will happen next?" Older students can use text, character development, chapter titles, and the book jackets to help make accurate predictions about what to expect. As teachers, we should not only encourage children to make such predictions, but later help them reflect upon and examine the accuracy of those predictions. Remember to ask, "What was it in the picture (text, title, etc.) that helped you predict that?" You may be surprised as you hear the many clues students see that often we, as adults, overlook!

As teachers share Janet Steven's (1995) *Tops and Bottoms*, you will find children eager to speculate about how Hare will trick Bear yet one more time. Other books which encourage hypothesizing and problem solving include figuring out who is the "denture thief" in *Grandpa's Teeth* (Clement, 1998); finding a way to get the cow down from the sky in Johnson's (1993) *The Cow Who Wouldn't Come Down*; and solving the bad breath problem of Haly, the Tosis family dog, in Dav Pilkey's (1994) *Dog Breath*. Give your students the chance to investigate and make assumptions based on prior knowledge and background information as they solve the hilarious mysteries in these and other books.

As we use books with all ages of children, we can help them make sense of their world in terms of the logical and sequential order of events. Chronological order plays an important part in many of the stories we read to children. In the *Little Old Woman Who Was Not Afraid of Anything* (Williams, 1988) the sequence of events (in creating a scarecrow) is very important. This sequential plot construction tells us that as she walks along the dark path she first meets a pair of pants, a shirt, and is followed by gloves, a hat, and finally a scary pumpkin head that says "Booooooo."

Often pourquoi tales, or "why" stories as they are commonly known, also depict a sequential series of events. For instance, Verna Aardema's (1975) *Why Mosquitoes Buzz in Peoples Ears: A West African Tale* describes the sequence of events which prevented the owl from waking the sun. Another example is seen in classic cumulative folktales such as *Drummerhoff* (Emberly, 1967) and *Fat Cat* (Kent, 1978). Other picture books with strong sequencial plots include *Snake Alley Band* (Nygaard, 1998) and *Lilly's Purple Plastic Purse* (Henkes, 1996).

In the sequential and cumulative structure of *Fat Cat*, children can see the story building from simple to much more complex. Although it begins with a cat and an old woman cooking her gruel, it quickly builds to include Skohottentot, Skolinkenlot, five birds in a flock, seven dancing girls, a lady with a parasol, the parson with the crooked staff, and finally, the woodcutter. Stories with a strong sequential organization are wonderful choices for Reader's Theater, creative dramatics, or retelling through flannel board figures. As children retell the events of the story, they begin to perfect their own skills of organizing.

A group of third grade students enjoyed the story *Three Cool Kids* (Emberly, 1995) so much, they asked their teacher if they could write a Reader's Theater script. This is a wonderfully funny story that offers a modern twist to the old Norwegian tale of the *Three Billy Goats Gruff*. The children had a great deal of interest in Reader's Theater since they and their teacher, Miss Ford, had performed some Reader's Theater scripts previously. The children understood that the format of Reader's Theater was like that of a play with characters assigned to read certain parts. They also knew that voices were very important and that reading with good expression and taking on the role of the character was critical. The teacher reported that during their previous experiences with Reader's Theater, they "had read like they had never read before with amazing fluency and expression!"

Today the class was taking the idea beyond what they had done in the past. They asked their teacher if they could write their own Reader's Theater script and perform it for the rest of the class. Using the book and the sequence of events in the plot as their guide, these hard working third graders created a wonderful product that was enjoyed by all a few days later. Figure 1.3 shows part of their script which the teacher typed for the children. See chapter 6 for many more examples of activities that support the skill of organizing.

Have you ever been asked to summarize something only to discover it is not as easy as it first appears. In summarizing, we must know the content and be able to select the most important points to make the summary clear clear and concise.

Summarizing skills can be developed and improved with literature of any genre and with children of any age. Whether considering "What part of the story did you like best?" or "Tell about the most exciting part of what you've read," being asked to think about the whole and reduce it to the most accurate and important features is a skill that can be honed through the use of children's literature.

Figure 1.3. Three Cool Kids

The Story of Three Cool Kids
Written by Eight Cool Kids

Narrator: Because they couldn't agree they stayed on the lot where the grass was about to run out. They hoped it would get better, but it didn't. Then one day, they noticed that there was only one puny weed left growing. The goats had to make a decision.

Middle: There's nothing left to eat. We've got to go for it.

Little: Yea, who cares about a rat. I'm hungry. I can almost taste that tender green grass across the street. Let's go.

Big: I think we have no choice. I'm not afraid. Let's go.

Narrator: So off went the three goats. They stopped at the corner before crossing the street. Their noses twitched. They could smell the sweet grass and they got even more excited.

Little: I'll go first. I'm not afraid.

Narrator: Little hopped off the curb and started across the street. Just then, he heard a terrible noise.

Rat: Who's making that terrible noise on my street?

Little: It's only me, Little Cool.

Rat: UMMMM. You smell like a good lunch.

Little: Boy are you rude! I'm not going to be YOUR lunch. Why do you want me anyway? I'm so little and there isn't much meat on my bones. I think you should wait for my big sister. She'll be along soon and she's a better lunch than I am.

Narrator: The rat liked the idea so he decided to wait. Middle soon came along.

Rat: Who's making that awful noise on my street?

Why not bring a little life and fun back to book reports in your classroom? Revise that old written book report format that calls on kids to begin with "The name of the book I read was . . . The author was . . ." and we all know the rest includes setting, main characters, and plot. B-O-R-I-N-G! Most teachers enjoy listening to them or reading them as little as their students enjoy preparing or delivering them. Why not grab the attention of your class while encouraging the refinement of summarizing skills with 60 second book commercials or book talks. If you'd like students to use props, which can make it even more exciting, call them book jackdaws (see chapter 5). Let your class create their own daytime talk show to interview the characters from a book. As the talk show guests, these characters give us an inside view of their thoughts and actions and help us understand the literary elements.

Recently I visited a fourth grade class which was presenting talk shows. One group had a show simply called Rachel! (they later told the audience that it was a take off on Oprah) another group called their show Chaz and Beth Ann (obviously taken from Regis and Kathy Lee), and a third group was led by a boy named David and his show was naturally called the David Betterman Show!

Another way to encourage summarization and research skills would be to utilize the setting of a book to direct a student or group of students to create a travelogue about that location. Jean Merrill's adaptation of *The Girl Who Loved Caterpillars* (1992) takes place in Japan; Eve Bunting's *Dandelions* (1995) follows a family who traveled across America's Great Plains in hopes of making a new home in a new land; John Steptoe's (1987) lovely tale, *Mufaro's Beautiful Daughters*, brings Africa's Zimbabwe region to readers everywhere; and Jan Brett's (1995) *Armadillo Rodeo* offers the reader scenes of western life in Texas.

Once each student selects a story, reads it, and identifies its setting, they can begin to research and explore that area of the world through a wide variety of resources. They become the travel agent who is a regional expert. Children will love being the expert and will enjoy sharing their information with the class or with other classes who may be studying that geographic location or are interested in learning more about it. This is especially fun to do during the second week in November which is National Geography Awareness Week.

However you and your children design the activity, it requires students to read the book, know the story well, understand the characters and their development, and be able to summarize the information in order to present it in this new and different format using all language modalities—reading, writing, thinking, speaking, and listening. It calls upon the reader to respond personally to the literature. Why not try it? You might enjoy it as much as your students do!

Books offer each of us a plethora of information; but do we have opportunities to apply this new information and knowledge in our real life situations? Books can provide those kinds of opportunities for children. Books cannot take the place of real experiences, but they can supplement and enhance them. When children in Mr. Russell's second grade class read *Wanda's Roses* (Brisson, 1994) they met the young girl who aspires to make her neighborhood a nicer, cleaner, and more beautiful place. We can integrate this message of care of the environment and the need for each of us to do our part into our own community into other content areas. Why not design a classroom project that helps children put these messages into real life practice? After reading Lynn Cherry's (1992) *A River Ran Wild*, Mr. Costa's fourth grade class wrote environmental radio announcements and read them on the local radio station. The lessons they learned through the book and the many discussions that followed were put into practice through this valuable community service project.

After Mrs. Beryl's kindergarten class heard Lois Ehlert's *Eating the Alphabet: Fruits and Vegetables A to Z* (1989), she realized that many of the children had never seen or tried a number of the fruits and vegetables in the book including the kiwi, asparagus, eggplant, and okra (to name just a few of the seventy-five fruits and vegetables included). Mrs. Beryl and her class created a semester long project that included reviewing the letters of the alphabet and a little cooking and plenty of tasting. This activity gave those young students a much better appreciation of fruits, vegetables, and letters of the alphabet by applying their new knowledge in a very real way—seeing and tasting a unique fruit or vegetable each day.

None of us, whether adult or child, should accept all that we hear or read without critical evaluation. Children must understand that bias can exist in the things we read. Critical thinking and evaluation are skills that require practice. Teachers can encourage criticizing, critical thinking, and problem solving through the kinds of questions we ask children.

Often the questions posed by reading a textbook series ask more low level and rote types of questions in which children simply give back information from the story such as "What did Toad do to help him remember things?" This encourages very convergent, narrow thinking. Teachers can offer more open ended questions that encourage divergent thinking and the use of higher level thinking skills. Start by reducing the number of "yes" or "no" or other one word answer questions. Give children a real chance to think with questions like "What would you have done after your friends left, if you had been Luke?" and "What else might the little red hen have done to get her friends to help her?" Notice that in this type of questioning, multiple responses are encouraged and real thinking, not merely the recitation of information, is expected.

By supporting students in their consideration of other possible solutions and by facilitating discussions that examine the authenticity of plots, characters, and settings of reading selections, we are encouraging children to develop their critical thinking skills.

Let's visit the very type of literature activity that promotes real learning and application of prior knowledge in Ms. Rice's second grade class. She had just started to read the book *The Cow Who Wouldn't Come Down* (Johnson, 1993). After only a few pages of reading, she stopped abruptly. "What is Miss Rosemary's problem?" she asked her attentively listening students. Desiree raised her hand quickly and announced with many giggles, "She has a flying cow and she won't come down from the sky." "So, continued Ms. Rice, "what can she do to solve this problem?"

Hands began waving all around the room, but Ms. Rice instead broke the class into five groups and asked them to share their ideas within their group and write them down. While they worked, she prepared a large chart on the board. She called it "The Solutions Chart." Following the brainstorming session, she had the groups share some of their best solutions to Miss Rosemary's "cow in the sky" problem. As they gave their ideas, Ms. Rice wrote them in the boxes across the chart.

"Wow, we have a lot of ideas," Ms. Rice concluded, "But do you think they are all good solutions to Miss Rosemary's problem? The class shouted out a resounding "No," as they laughed. There were indeed some fairly creative responses. The class began to discuss why some would not work well.

As the class pointed out such things as "that idea's really dangerous," or "you'd need stuff a lady on a farm doesn't have," or "that idea would never work," Ms. Rice recorded these thoughts down the left side of the chart. She then moved on to a discussion of the importance of considering all possible solutions and the good and bad things about each one before selecting the best solution. Using the chart, the class evaluated how possible and realistic each idea would be. By assigning a numerical value to each idea as it related to danger, chance of success, and needed materials, they decided to discard several ideas (including using the fire company's ladder truck, a helicopeter with a rescue rope, and the hot air balloon idea, too). The class decided that the best solution seemed to be putting out a large amount of Gertrude's most favorite food. As L.J. pointed out, "What cow could ignore that?" What Ms. Rice created from the ideas of the students is shown in Figure 1.4.

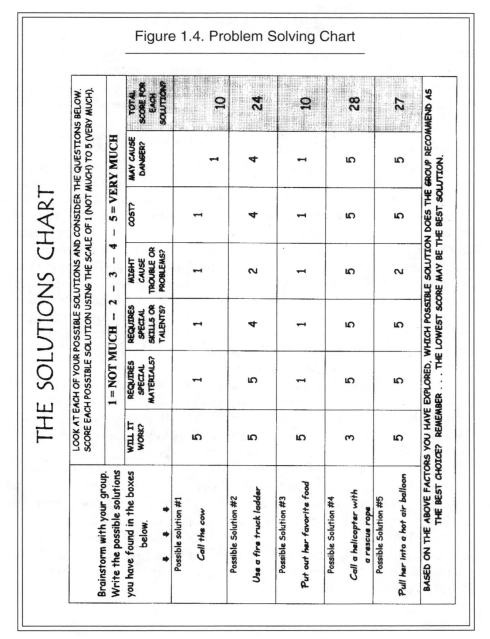

Figure 1.4. Problem Solving Chart

THE SOLUTIONS CHART

LOOK AT EACH OF YOUR POSSIBLE SOLUTIONS AND CONSIDER THE QUESTIONS BELOW. SCORE EACH POSSIBLE SOLUTION USING THE SCALE OF 1 (NOT MUCH) TO 5 (VERY MUCH).

1 = NOT MUCH – 2 – 3 – 4 – 5 = VERY MUCH

Brainstorm with your group. Write the possible solutions you have found in the boxes below.

	WILL IT WORK?	REQUIRES SPECIAL MATERIALS?	REQUIRES SPECIAL SKILLS OR TALENTS?	MIGHT CAUSE TROUBLE OR PROBLEMS?	COST?	MAY CAUSE DANGER?	TOTAL SCORE FOR EACH SOLUTION?
Possible solution #1 — Call the cow	5	1	1	1	1	1	10
Possible Solution #2 — Use a fire truck ladder	5	5	4	2	4	4	24
Possible Solution #3 — Put out her favorite food	5	1	1	1	1	1	10
Possible Solution #4 — Call a helicopter with a rescue rope	3	5	5	5	5	5	28
Possible Solution #5 — Pull her into a hot air balloon	5	5	5	2	5	5	27

BASED ON THE ABOVE FACTORS YOU HAVE EXPLORED, WHICH POSSIBLE SOLUTION DOES THE GROUP RECOMMEND AS THE BEST CHOICE? REMEMBER . . . THE LOWEST SCORE MAY BE THE BEST SOLUTION.

This teacher gave her class an opportunity to be real thinkers and consider multiple possibilities through applying what they already knew from their life experiences. There are a number of other excellent stories that lend themselves to using problem-solving skills. A few of my other personal favorites include *Tom's Tail* (Jennings, 1995), the story of a young pig who's curly-twirly tail present quite a problem, Margie Palatini's

Moosetache (1997) in which the Moose's very long and bothersome "moosetache" is problematic as it gets in the way of everything he most enjoys doing, and the fun mystery of who took grandpa's dentures in *Grandpa's Teeth* (Clement, 1998). Try exploring these books and the many others that encourage students of all ages to identify multiple solutions in an effort to determine the best way to solve a problem.

What Research Tells Us

By now you are probably thinking, "Sure, all of this sounds great, but can it be substantiated? Does reading research support the value of using literature with children?" Studies have been conducted in classrooms where literature is the foundation of the reading program. In many of these classrooms, children who had not done well with literacy learning were now experiencing success with literature-based programs. A study, conducted by Cullinan, Jaggar, and Strickland (1974) compared the growth of two groups. One was taught using a literature approach and the other a more traditional basal method. The literature group showed significant improvement over the basal reader group in a number of areas including word knowledge, comprehension, and quality of vocabulary. Other studies that show similar findings include Larrick (1987) and Roser, Hoffman, and Farest (1990).

Additional research supports various components of a literature-rich environment including the value of reading aloud (Cramer, 1975, and Trelease, 1989); forming a community of readers (Hepler and Hickman, 1982); and immersion and authenticity (Goodman, 1986; Atwell, 1987; Cambourne, 1988; and Smith, 1989).

Personally, I don't believe there is a single thing that can't be taught through literature. After reading this book, you will have to decide if you agree with me or not. Is it always easy? No, because the prepared materials produced in great volumes by book companies are so well packaged and seemingly inclusive that little could be easier than that. But do I believe it is better for our children to use real stories and authentic learning experiences as the basis for their learning? You better believe I do. Let's see what you think.

References

Anderson, A. B., Teale, W. H., & Estrada, E. (1980). Low income children's pre-school literacy experiences: Some naturalistic observation. *Quarterly Newsletters of the Laboratory of Comparative Human Cognition, 2*, 59–65.

Atwell, N. (1987). *In the middle: Writing, reading, and learning with adolescents.* Portsmouth, NH: Heinemann.

Bishop, R. S. (1997). Extending multicultural understanding through children's books. In B. E. Cullinan (Ed.), *Children's literature in the reading program* (pp. 60–67). Newark, DE: International Reading Association.

Cambourne, B. (1988). *The whole story: Natural learning and the acquisition of literacy in the classroom.* Richmond-Hill, Ontario: Scholastic-TAB.

Cramer, R. L. (1975). Reading to children: Why and how. *The Reading Teacher, 28,* 460–463.

Cullinan, B. (1981). *Literature and the child.* New York: Harcourt Brace Jovanovich.

Cullinan, B., Jagger, A., & Strickland, D. (1974). Language expansion for black children in primary grades. A research report. *Young Children, 29,* 98–112.

Dale, P. (1976). *Language development.* New York: Holt, Rinehart, and Winston.

Ford, M. T. (1994, July 18). The cult of multiculturalism. *Publishers Weekly,* pp. 30–33.

Goodman, K. (1982). Comprehension-centered reading instruction. In F. Gollasch (Ed.), *Language and literacy: The selected writings of Kenneth Goodman* (pp. 75–86). London: Routledge and Kegan Paul.

Goodman, K. (1986). *What's whole in whole language.* Portsmouth, NH: Heinemann.

Hepler, S. I. & Hickman, J. (1982). The book was okay. I love you—Social aspects of response to literature. *Theory into Practice, 21,* 278–283.

Horning, K. T. & Kruse, G. M. (1991). Looking into the mirror: Considerations behind the reflections. In M. V. Lindgren (Ed.), *The multicultural mirror: Cultural substances in literature for children and young adults* (pp. 1–13). Fort Atkinson, WI: Highsmith Press.

Jalongo, M. R. (1988). *Young children and picture books: Literature from infancy to six.* Washington, D. C.: National Association for the Education of Young Children.

Larrick, N. (1965). The all-white world of children's books. *Saturday Review, 48,* 63–64, 84–85.

Larrick, N. (1987). Literacy starts too soon. *Phi Delta Kappan, 69,* 184–189.

Loban, W. (1976). *Language development: Kindergarten through grade twelve.* Urbana, IL: National Council of Teachers of English.

O'Malley, J. (1997). Considering the sources and the resources. *Book Links, 6,* 5.

Roser, N. L., Hoffman, J. V., & Farest, C. (1990). Language, literature, and at-risk children. *The Reading Teacher, 43,* 554–561.

Ruddman, M. K. & Pearce, A. M. (1988). *For love of reading: A parent's guide for encouraging young readers from literacy through age 5.* Mount Vernon, NY: Consumers Union.

Smith, F. (1989). Demonstrations, engagements, and sensitivity. The choice between people and programs. In Manning, G. & Manning, M. (Eds.) *Whole language: Beliefs and practices, K–8*. Washington, DC: National Education Association.

Trelease, J. (1989). *The new read-aloud handbook*. New York: Penguin.

Children's Books

Aardema, V. (1975). *Why mosquitoes buzz in people's ears: A West African tale*. Illus. Leo & Diane Dillon. New York: Dial.

Adler, D. (1998). *The many troubles of Andy Russell*. New York: Harcourt Brace & Company.

Anderson, H. C. (1982). *The emperor's new clothes*. New York: Harper.

Bateman, R. (1998). *Safari*. New York: Little, Brown and Company.

Barton, B. (1991). *The three bears*. New York: Harper.

Bourgeois, P. (1986). *Franklin in the dark*. Toronto, Ontario: Kids Can Press.

Brett, J. (1995). *Armadillo rodeo*. New York: Putnam.

Brisson, P. (1994). *Wanda's roses*. Illus. Maryann Cocca-Leffler. Honesdale, PA: Boyds Mills.

Buehner, C. (1996). *Fanny's dream*. Illus. Mark Buehner. New York: Dial.

Bunting, E. (1991). *Fly away home*. Illus. Ronald Himler. New York: Clarion.

Bunting, E. (1995). *Dandelions*. Illus. Greg Shed. San Diego: Harcourt.

Calmenson, S. (1989). *The principal's new clothes*. Illus. Denise Brunkus. New York: Scholastic.

Cameron (1987). *The stories Julian tells*. New York: Knopf.

Cherry, L. (1992). *A river ran wild*. New York: Dutton.

Cherry, L. (1995). *Armadillo rodeo*. New York: Putnam.

Christelow, E. (1990). *Five little monkeys jumping on the bed*. Boston: Clarion.

Cleary, B. (1965). *The mouse and the motorcycle*. New York: William Morrow.

Clement, R. (1998) *Grandpa's teeth*. New York: HarperCollins.

Conrad, P. (1988). *Staying nine*. New York: Harper Row.

Dahl, R. (1961). *James and the giant peach*. Illus. Nancy Ekholm Burkett. New York: Knopf.

Dahl, R. (1982). *The BFG*. New York: Farrar, Straus & Giroux.

Ehlert, L. (1989). *Eating the alphabet*. New York: Harcourt.

Emberley, B. (1967). *Drummerhoff*. Illus. Ed Emberley. Englewood Cliffs, NJ: Prentice.

Emberly, R. (1995). *Three cool kids*. New York: Little, Brown and Company.

Galdone, P. (1985). *The little red hen*. Boston: Clarion.

Giff, P. R. (1985). *The beast in Mrs. Rooney's room*. New York: Dell.

Grimm, J., & Grimm, W. (1992). *The Bremen town musicians*. Illus. Bernadette Watts. New York: North-South.

Hautzig, D. (1996). *Pedal power: How a mountain bike is made*. New York: Lodestar.

Henkes, K. (1990). *Julius, the baby of the world*. New York: Greenwillow.

Henkes, K. (1996). *Lilly's purple plastic purse*. New York: Greenwillow.

Hoban, T. (1983). *Exactly the opposite*. New York: Greenwillow.

Hoban, T. (1995). *Colors everywhere*. New York: Greenwillow.

Hoban, T. (1985). *Is it larger? Is it smaller*. New York: Greenwillow.

Hoffman, M. (1991). *Amazing Grace*. New York: Dial.

Jennings, L. (1995) *Tom's tail*. New York: Little, Brown and Company.

Johnson, P. B. (1993). *The cow who wouldn't come down*. New York: Orchard.

Johnson, S. (1994). *Alphabet city*. New York: Viking.

Johnson, S. (1999). *City by numbers*. New York: Viking.

Juster, N. (1961). *The phantom tollbooth*. New York: Random House.

Kellogg, S. (1986). *Best friends*. New York: Dial.

Kent, J. (1978). *Fat cat*. New York: Scholastic Books.

Kimmel, E. (1993). *The gingerbread man*. Illus. Megan Lloyd. New York: Holiday.

Komaiko, L. (1997). *Annie Bananie: Best friends to the end*. New York: Bantam Doubleday Dell.

Kraus, R. (1994). *Leo the late bloomer*. Illus. Jose Aruego. New York: HarperCollins.

MacLachlan, P. (1985). *Sarah, plain and tall*. New York: Harper & Row.

Marshall, J. (1995). *Look once, look twice*. New York: Ticknor & Fields.

McCloskey, R. (1941). *Make way for ducklings*. New York: Viking.

Merrill, J. (1992). *The girl who loved caterpillars*. Illus. Floyd Cooper. New York: Putnam.

Mosel, A. (1968). *Tikki Tikki Tembo*. Illus. Blair Lent. Austin, TX: Holt, Rinehart & Winston.

Nygaard, E. (1998). *Snake alley band*. Illus. Betsy Lewin. New York: Doubleday.

Palatine, M. (1997). *Moosetache*. New York: Scholastic.

Parish, P. (1992). *Amelia Bedelia*. Illus. Fritz Siebel. New York: HarperCollins.

Paterson, K. 1978). *The great Gilly Hopkins*. New York: Crowell.

Perrault, C. (1954). *Cinderella*. Illus. Marcia Brown. New York: Scribner's.

Pilkey, D. (1994). *Dog breath*. New York: Scholastic.

Pinkney, A. D.(1995). *Hold fasts to your dreams*. New York: Morrow.

Polacco, P. (1998). *Thank you, Mr. Falker*. New York: Philomel.

Raskin, E. (1978). *The westing game*. New York: Dutton.

Rey, H. A. (1941). *Curious George*. Boston: Houghton.

Ringgold, F. (1991). *Tar beach*. New York: Crown.

Rylant, C. (1992). *Missing May*. New York: Orchard.

Scieszka, J. (1993). *Your mother was a Neanderthal*. New York: Viking.

Sendak, M. (1963). *Where the wild things are*. New York: Harper.

Steptoe, J. (1987). *Mufaro's beautiful daughters: An African tale*. New York: Lothrop.

Stevens, J. (1995). *Tops and bottoms*. New York: Harcourt Brace.

Stiner, J. (1999). *Look-alikes*. New York: Little, Brown and Company.

Turner, A. (1997). *Mississippi mud: Three prairie journals*. New York: HarperCollins.

Van Allsburg, C. (1990). *Just a dream*. Boston: Houghton Mifflin.

Viorst, J. (1972). *Alexander and the terrible, horrible, no good, very bad day*. New York: Atheneum.

Vozar, D. (1998). *Rapunzel: A happenin' rap*. Illus. Betsy Lewin. New York: Bantam Doubleday Dell.

Waber, B. (1972). *Ira sleeps over*. New York: Houghton Mifflin.

White, E. B. (1952). *Charlotte's web*. Illus. Garth Williams. New York: Harper.

Williams, L. (1988), *The little old lady who was not afraid of anything*. Illus. Megan Lloyd. New York: HarperTrophy.

Williams, M. (1922, 1991). *The velveteen rabbit*. Illus. William Nicholson. New York: Doubleday.

Wood, A. (1984). *The napping house*. Illus. Don Wood. San Diego: Harcourt.

2

A Response-Centered, Literature-Rich Classroom

"Are you going to read everything in that bag, Mama?", Dad asks her. He's grinning, but his eyes are brimming over with tears and he and Mom are holding hands across the table.

"Maybe I will read everything in the world now that I've started," Grandma says in a stuck-up way. "I've got time."

Eve Bunting, 1989, p. 26

Is Your Classroom Literature-Rich?

Just as Grandma enjoyed sharing and showing her newly developed skill of reading, each of us who discovers something we value will proudly display it in our own way. We talk about it, add new examples to our collections, and make it a part of our lives. Those of us who value literature, line our walls with books. We hear a voice calling us into the bookstore as we walk through shopping malls. It is hauntingly real. Our love of books calls us in to browse, read, and of course, spend a few more dollars on books. We share new books and favorite ideas with our friends, colleagues, sometimes even those who have no connections with children's literature at all! They may look strangely at us at first, but they humor us and allow us to share our enthusiasm. We especially share great books with children. We have an insatiable desire for books and some of us find we cannot stop until we have just one more!

Those of us who enjoy books and use literature in teaching offer children a literate environment—a classroom that is literature-rich. What is a literate environment? To what degree do you personally provide your students with an environment rich in literary experiences and materials? Cox and Zarillo (1993) describe the components of a literate environment to include nine elements. Figure 2.1 lists both the elements of a literate environment (on the left) and those activities that describe the element (on the right).

Figure 2.1
Elements of a Literate Environment

1. Provide Books in the Environment	A space in which many books are available and accessible for children's use.
2. Reading Materials Which are Appropriate for Children	Teachers should select reading materials that their students can read and those which are developmentally appropriate for the age. These should include a variety of formats including books, magazines, newspapers, and audio, video, and CD ROMS.
3. Somebody to Read to the Child	Every child can benefit from a good model. Teachers, parents, siblings, grandparents, classroom volunteers, and older students should read aloud to children.
4. An Adult to Help	Adults can and should help children by reading aloud and by responding to the child's natural curiosity. Questions like, "What is that?" and "Why did she do that?" will result from interactions with literature. What is important is that adults respond to children and their questions.
5. Provide a Model of Proficiency	Allow children to see you as a successful reader. This means children see you reading both silently and orally in your everyday life, enjoying reading, learning from reading, and using reading as a tool to answer questions and solve problems.
6. Writing Tools	Since there is a strong interrelationship between reading and writing, teachers should provide a variety of tools—pens, paper, pencils, markers, and computers.
7. Literacy As a Tool to Give and Get Meaning	Print is a powerful tool that gives and sends messages to others. We learn words through using words, and the words we use carry meaning.

cont.

8. Time to Read Silently	We do not learn how to read without practicing. Children need time to read silently if they are to improve. They will get better at reading because they read. Give children time to self-select the book they want to read and time to read every day in your classroom. And remember, teachers should read during SSR, too!
9. A Wide Range of Experiences	Many years ago, John Dewey discovered that we learn through hands-on experience. The more a child experiences literature first hand the better reader he will become.
Note: Adapted with permission from Cox and Zarillo (1993)	

As you review this set of criteria, do you see yourself demonstrating and providing to your literacy learners all nine of these elements? If not, can you find ways in which you can achieve a more literate environment in your classroom by more effectively incorporating these nine criteria?

A Literature-Rich Environment

A visit to two literature-rich classrooms will help demonstrate the components of a literature-rich classroom.

Mrs. Owens' Classroom

Mrs. Marilyn Owens has hundreds of books all around her classroom in a small rural school where she has taught for 17 years. She has shelves of books everywhere, seemingly made from everything from milk crates to bricks and boards. The message is clear, "Books and reading are important in this classroom."

Marilyn also has materials (paper, pencils, crayons, markers, and computers) that encourage and facilitate her second graders to write their stories. The children's work is displayed on a bulletin board titled "Stories We Have Written." There is also a clothes line with pinch clothespins for hanging their art work related to their literary experiences.

Additionally, the room itself speaks out to the reader. It offers comfortable places to sit and read from a decorated refrigerator box to a small wooden jungle gym which has been slightly modified and redecorated. It bears a child-made sign that reads, "The Reading Loft." The other classroom furniture is arranged in clusters. Not that everything these children do is organized as a group activity, but this teacher believes that education, and specifically reading, is a social process and that her room must support such partner or group activities. There are also small group discussion areas where children gather to "talk" about what they are reading. Often with Marilyn, but at other times just with each other.

Every day the class enjoys 15 minutes of DEAR (Drop Everything and Read); and during this time, everyone including Marilyn, reads. The message again is clear that reading plays an important role for everyone including the teacher.

Mr. Verdet's Classroom

In another school, this one large and urban and far from the small community in which Marilyn teaches, we find Mr. Tyrell Verdet's group of second grade students. Tyrell has been teaching for four years and clearly enjoys the time he spends in his classroom. He seems to move around the room as if his movements were choreographed. He is the epitome of the teacher who really has his finger on the pulse of his classroom.

The arrangement of the room is somewhat different than Marilyn's, yet it is obvious that books play a very big role. There are a few teacher created bulletin boards, but many more displays of children's work—pictures, stories, and hand-made crafts. There are also plenty of children's books and journals neatly stacked on shelves. These children respond to what they are reading in response journals each day. They also have personal journals in which they write each morning telling of particular events which might have transpired since the previous day's entry.

These children are always actively involved in what they read, whether they are dressing up as book characters and telling about themselves, singing original songs about the literature they were reading, writing letters to authors, or making reading bumper stickers. Tyrell's classroom is buzzing with literature related activities. Even when a stranger enters the room, there is a child anxious to read to that visitor, share with them the current response activity of the day, or ask them to grab a book and read, too! Tyrell praises the children often and talks and acts so positively about books that his enthusiasm is clearly contagious. Since many of his students don't have books at home, he has organized a read-at-home program that makes it possible for children to take books home each evening. He is providing for what their environment clearly lacks, and they are loving it and learning from it.

Although these two second grade classrooms appear in sharp contrast to each other in some ways, they are certainly both literature-rich environments where teachers use literature in various ways and for various purposes throughout the day. Similarities show that many books are accessible to all students. There is variety in the books available from fantasy to biography and poetry to historical fiction (both teachers rely heavily on their school library to help provide the many books they display). The children's work is proudly displayed. Literature is integrated into other subject areas throughout the day, and those subjects are also integrated into reading instruction. The physical environment is conducive to the required movement when students engage in literary responses and learners are no longer confined to sitting in their desks and raising their hands to talk (although there are times throughout the day when this is appropriate and expected). These teachers experiment with use of space and "try on" different ideas. In both classrooms, the room is divided into areas or centers (i.e., the writing center, the art center, the library center, and the discussion area).

In these examples, we see how two very different teachers have created very rich, literature-centered environments to facilitate the development, learning, and enjoyment of children. Think of your own classroom. Write a description telling about those features that make your own classroom a rich, literature-centered environment for children.

What Do You Mean by Response Centered?

We have all had responses to literature. Think about the last book you read. Was there something in the book you wanted to share with someone? That was a response. Think about the pictures that formed in your mind as you read the book. You were visualizing—a type of response. Think about that exciting moment when you thought you knew what would happen next—the anticipation of the event or the character's behavior. You were making predictions and that was a type of response. Think about what you did at the end of the book. You loved it. You hated it. You announced, "That was a terrific book," or thought "That book was not what I had hoped it would be! What a waste of my time." Those comments you articulated to others or kept to yourself were responses to literature.

Goforth (1998) describes the process of responding to literature as containing three components which she calls the "Three C's." When we respond we are *connected* with the ideas offered by the author or illustrator as well as with our own prior experiences. Once this occurs, we *construct* meaning of our own as a result of the reflection on those ideas and images. Lastly, we *create* pictures in our mind's eye of the events we have read about and go on to create our own responses. This is a time of active visualization. It is through these responses to the text that personal meaning is evoked.

So how does this process occur with the children we teach? As teachers, when we share a book with children, we can easily offer the reader/listener the opportunity to connect through the questions we ask and the opportunities we offer them to respond in an active and personal way. Encourage children to "hook into" their prior knowledge and background and stimulate their connections through opportunities to talk with each other in an organized way. "Have you ever had anything like this happen to you?" or "What might you have done differently to solve the problem?" Encourage the reader/listener to make predictions, solve problems, bring their own experiences to the story to facilitate making connections.

Having made a number of connections of one's own and having heard some of the thoughts and experiences of others helps the child be ready to "construct." Your students can clarify their understanding of the story through retelling or responding to questions that prompt higher level thinking. Try to get away from questions with one word answers so often offered by the teacher's guide of the basal reader. Rather than asking "What did Jeremy really want for his birthday?" you might ask, "Now that you know what Jeremy wanted for his birthday, what do you think might have been a more practical gift and why?" Notice how this question calls upon the student to use what she comprehended from the story as well as some of her own ideas and opinions. Because the question calls for a "why," the student is required to support, justify, and elaborate on the answer. These kinds of questions allow students to bring a whole new dimension to story discussion and the construction of meaning.

Students will eagerly engage in the challenge of using different language modalities including reading, speaking, writing, listening, and thinking to develop creative responses to what they have read. These activities call upon students to bring more of themselves to the activity. They must still have and draw upon a good understanding of the text, but now they become active participants in the story rather than passive recipients of information. Whether they are creating an advertisement for the book, a wanted poster of their favorite or least favorite character, a public service radio announcement connected to the theme of a story, puppets to recreate the tale, or a personal biography following the reading of a biography of a famous person, their enthusiastic responses may astound you! It is this kind of active student engagement that this book advocates as the primary purpose for using literature in the classroom. Chapter 6 offers over 80 ideas to more completely engage students in the books they read. But why? What is wrong with the way I've done it for years?

Why Change the Way You Teach?

Some of you might shake your heads and question the notion of active involvement as did Dee, a fourth grade teacher with sixteen years in the classroom. Dee's comment was simple and to the point when she asked, "What is wrong with what I have been doing?" She went on to say, "For years I have used literature in some way in my classroom. I believe I have been relatively successful, and I have never worried about the active involvement of my students. I have introduced the vocabulary words to every piece of literature, we have worked with the words, looked up definitions, used them in sentences, and had a quiz to test our word knowledge. The students have read the story and we've talked about it. I've also identified a number of skills to which each book lends itself, and I have taught specific reading skills as a part of the book activity. I have spent a great deal of time creating worksheets to test their comprehension and understanding of these skills, and they have received a grade just as they did with the basal. What do you mean by 'active participant rather than passive recipient?' You know the old adage, 'if it ain't broke, don't fix it.' I don't think there's a thing wrong with the way I use literature."

The purpose of this book is not to point out what may be "wrong" with one's teaching or method of using literature. What it is designed to hopefully do is cause each of us to think differently about how we can more effectively use literature in our classrooms, to ensure improvement in language arts (reading, speaking, writing, and listening) and to engage children in positive experiences which will facilitate their interest in and continued encounters with books. That is, creating lifelong readers! Literature is a wonderful diversion from the step-by-step progression of the commercial reading series. If we consider all the values of literature discussed in chapter 1, we can see that it has so much to offer all of us. Part of the problem in reading classrooms, is that so many students have had some less than positive experiences with reading.

How can we achieve our goal of transforming children into lifelong readers rather than simply good readers during reading class? We can only do this if teachers make books exciting and engaging, interesting and fun, extensions of real life, and passages to new worlds. This can most easily happen if we allow children to experience books through active participation. It is through these kinds of hands-on connections that they see themselves as active participants rather than the passive recipients that worksheets, workbooks, and many pencil and paper activities offer. This is not to say that we stop teaching children to read or that decoding words, comprehension, and other reading skills are not important—they certainly are. It is to say that we can make books and the work we do with books appealing to students, so that they look forward to working with them again and again.

Years ago when I was an adolescent, I recall my mother saying, "It's the parsley on the plate." Our conversation had nothing to do with books and reading and it had nothing to do with food and cooking. It was her way of describing the need to "dress" something up to make it more appealing. The way in which we have taught reading for years may not "be broken" but I believe it could benefit from a tune-up. While we must help children negotiate the symbol system of reading, we also need to "dress up" the process to make reading and literature appealing to them.

Responding to literature is natural and different for each of us. It is our way to reflect, relive a part of the book, share views with others, and make connections to other things we have read as well as our own lives. These responses allow the reader/listener to take a more active role in the understanding of the text than was traditionally allowed with commercially prepared programs. The way in which children respond as they read may be oral (a puppet show or sharing their reader's theater script); artistic (comic strip stories or designing a book jacket); manipulative (creating roller movies or playing a literature board game); or written (designing a fan letter to an author or illustrator or writing a book review for the school newspaper).

How children respond may be as different as the children themselves. Their responses are "artifacts" to be shared, displayed, and enjoyed by others. Their responses are not necessarily graded (in the traditional A, B, C, sense) but can support alternative forms of assessment. Literary responses can be individually selected by children based on their strengths or areas of interest. Bobby, a talented nine year-old who loves to draw, usually chooses an artistic response; while Marc, a very social and outgoing child, prefers responses that are oral and involve others.

As the teacher designing response activities for children, you may also select the response mode—written, artistic, manipulative, or oral. Often teachers use a mini-lesson format to prepare students for a selected literary response. For instance, after reading *Four Famished Foxes and Fosdyke* (Edwards, 1995), Evelyn Banner, a fourth grade teacher, gave a lesson on alliteration to prepare the children to write their own alliterative tales. Each child selected a letter of the alphabet and began writing a short story using alliteration and their selected letter. In Figure 2.2, you can read the story written by Danielle who chose the letter "D" because "it is the first letter in my name."

Figure 2.2. Danielle's Story

Dr. Dick Dawson went to the dog pound to get a Great Dane. Dr. Dick Dawson named the dog Doppy. Doppy was a dumb dog, he always got dirty. Doppy always digs up dandylions. Doppy's favorite dog food is Dibble Dog chow. Doppy was down when Dr. Dick Dawson said he was disloyal. One day Doppy was walking across the road and got hit by a Dodge. Doppy died December 14, 1998.

Teachers who have weaned themselves from the workbook that is typically associated with reading instruction will see numerous benefits when children respond actively to literature. A number of benefits that have been shared through conversations and interactions with classroom teachers are described in Figure 2.3.

Figure 2.3 What Teachers Think About Using Literature	
Michelle, Kindergarten Teacher	It is the foundation of everything we do in kindergarten. From a good book, I can teach a unit on any topic. I can use literature as my vehicle to teach language skills, math, social studies, science, you name it!
Bonnie, First Grade Teacher	For me it all comes down to the enthusiasm it generates. Using trade books allows me to demonstrate how reading is not just what we do with the reader between 9:45 and 11:00 each day. The message it allows me to convey to my students is that reading is getting enjoyment and meaning from print— all kinds of print.
Liz, Second Grade Teacher	My opinion has evolved over time. When I began teaching, I was stuck in teaching information. You know—facts in science, operations in math, word recognition in reading. But now I have a better sense of what learning is and it is so much more. It is being able to find and use information, and literature is one way I can help support their quest for new knowledge in a fun and appealing way. I still teach and work very hard, but I do it a lot differently today than I did in 1981. Using children's books has helped lead the way to that new way of teaching for me.
Tyrell, Third Grade Teacher	I can teach my students that their opinions matter as we discuss trade books. It is our connection with life and the real world and, because of literature, their world is a better place.
Bill, Fourth Grade Teacher	Provide excitement and enjoyment for my class—that's what trade books do for me. My students just love it when we leave the basal and use whole class sets of great books like *The Other Side of the Mountain* or *Hatchet*. Trade books offer this tough audience of fourth graders the incentive to read, and they love it!

Does all of this mean we don't need the workbook anymore? Does this mean teachers should not use the basal or other commercially produced reading series? Are you saying that what I have been doing all these years is wrong? The answer to each of these questions is clearly "NO!"

No, you do not need to throw out the workbooks that accompany your basal reading series. Simply understand that a workbook most often asks questions that encourages convergent thinking—one correct answer that serves as a "giving back" of story information. The questions encourage a literal interpretation of the story rather than higher level thinking skills and more divergent thinking. Having a good understanding of the story is important, but so are children who are good, creative thinkers. Recalling the name of the boy in the story will not help our students one bit in five, ten, or fifteen years, but being able to analyze and think critically and creatively will. When we ask a child to consider what a story character has done to solve his problem and to offer other suggestions that might work, we are encouraging the development of skills that will help a child for a lifetime.

Consider what one mother of a six year old said about reading and workbook usage. Although not a teacher in the formal sense, she understood children perhaps better than her son's teacher when she said,

> Something seems wrong with this picture. My first grade son
> who was simply thrilled about being able to read is now read-
> ing in his book for five minutes and then doing workbook pages
> and photocopied papers for the next 55 minutes of reading
> class. How can we call this *reading* class and how can we not
> kill his enthusiasm with a routine like this day in and day out?

Her point about the abuse of workbooks and worksheets was certainly clear. Think about your own classrooms. Do your children read only a few minutes and then do activities that require little reading or creative thinking for the remainder of class? As you decide what your students will do in class today, ask yourself what they will learn from that activity. As teachers we can easily fall prey to the "ease" of using a workbook and black line masters, but we need to stop and think about the value they do or don't offer our children.

Is assessing children's understanding important? Yes it certainly is. What I am suggesting is that teachers find ways to supplement the traditional workbook activities and of assessments with alternative ways of helping children develop the kinds of critical thinking skills that today's children and tomorrow's leaders need. Creating a response-centered classroom with authentic learning experiences encourages that kind of thinking and learning.

Circling the word that fits in the blank, coloring the circle that shows which vocabulary word works best in the sentence, circling a picture that begins with the same consonant cluster all check for understanding, but none allows children to do the kind of real thinking that will be needed in the 21st century. Sharing quality literature and providing children with activities that foster real thinking and doing does provide that and so much more.

The Profile of a Successful Literature Teacher

There are many successful literature teachers in classrooms across America. Many of them have made a real effort to provide literature and literature related experiences for their students. Others are simply doing what they enjoy—sharing great books with children in a variety of ways.

A successful literature teacher assumes several roles. This teacher is a reflective, informed professional who creates and models appropriate literature-based experiences for children. This individual encourages children's active involvement with books and respects the responses children offer. A successful literature teacher is one who is always open to suggestions and looks for better ways to share books with children. This teacher is always learning, growing, and changing. Figure 2.4 identifies some characteristics of successful literature teachers. How many of these traits do you see in yourself?

Figure 2.4
Characteristics of a Successful Literature Teacher

---

1. Shows enthusiasm toward children's books.

2. Models personal enjoyment of children's books.

3. Demonstrates an effective presentation of children's literature.

4. Realizes the importance of students exposure to a variety of genres.

5. Shares new books and book-related activities with other book lovers.

6. Considers the students' cultural backgrounds and experiences when exploring literature.

7. Considers issues of diversity not only in terms of race and culture, but also family, socioeconomic status, age, and gender in selecting books for children.

8. Arranges the classroom to facilitate the enjoyment and exploration of literature

9. Encourages children's active responses to literature.

10. Involves students in the selection of books and related activities.

11. Helps children as they connect, construct, and create their responses to literature.

References

Cox, C. & Zarrillo, J. (1993). *Teaching reading with children's literature*. New York: Macmillan.

Goforth, F. S. (1998). *Literature and the learner*. New York: Wadsworth.

Children's Books

Bunting, E. (1989). *The Wednesday surprise*. New York: Clarion.

Edwards, P. D. (1995). *Four famished foxes and Fosdyke*. New York: HarperCollins.

Part 2

Choosing and Using Literature

Part 2 gives teachers the opportunity to look closely at themselves and their beliefs. In chapter 3, "Before Bringing Children and Books Together" you will be asked to consider your own personal philosophy about how children learn. Does your teaching reflect your personal belief system? That is a question you will be pushed to consider and honestly answer as you read this chapter.

Some teachers may want to implement change immediately. You may find yourself flipping ahead to the activities offered in chapter 6, foregoing these preliminary chapters. I encourage you to first take time to consider the "whys" and the "hows." Why do you want to make changes in your teaching? Don't be the teacher who has not seriously examined or reexamined your beliefs about reading instruction, or one who has not taken a hard look at what you see as "best" for the children you teach. Too often, teachers make changes because someone else encourages it or everyone else is doing it. That is not enough! Know what you believe and allow those beliefs about teaching and learning to serve as the foundation for what you do in your reading program.

3

Before Bringing Children and Books Together

She always took a book to bed,
With a flashlight under the sheet
She'd make a tent of covers
And read herself to sleep.

Sarah Stewart, 1995, unnumbered

How Do We Learn to Read?

There are many children like the character described above who just can't be without a book. They take them everywhere—even to bed! But before children can make a cavern under the sheets and read their books with a flashlight, they must learn to read. How does that happen?

Look back for a moment to Ms. Owens' and Mr. Verdet's second grade classrooms described in chapter 2. In these examples of literacy-rich environments, how were children learning to read?

Some might say they are learning to read as a result of the excellent models their teachers provided. Others might attribute it to their numerous literacy experiences including many opportunities for exposure to print and opportunities to create and use print. Some might argue that someone must be providing these students with good, solid "reading instruction." Others would contend that these children, like all children, learn to read by doing what we all do, and that is striving to create meaning (Douglas, 1989). All of these suggestions would correctly describe "how" children learn to read not only in these classrooms, but how the process happens for children around the world.

Think for a moment about your own reading experiences or those of your own children. Do you remember reading as a child? How do you recall it happening? What do you remember about your reading instruction? Or your own children or those of a close friend—how did the advent of reading happen for them? Could that young child read before entering school and before formal reading instruction began? Think about children from your own classroom who are excellent readers or perhaps the child who struggles with reading. What do you believe to be the reason for this success or failure? Think about some or all of these questions before proceeding with this exploration of how and why we can bring books and children together.

Talking about reading can be very complicated, because we are reading all the time. You are doing it right now, although when we read we are not always reading words. We read the unhappy tone is someone's voice, the dark skies that indicate a storm is coming, the strategy of the pitcher as we think about stealing second base, the body language of a sad child or one who is about to burst if he doesn't tell you his good news! Douglas (1989) describes reading as "the process of creating meaning for any and everything in the environment for which the reader develops an awareness" (p. 27).

In recent years, this explanation of how we make meaning of our world and "read" has been called the constructivist learning theory. It is an active construction of knowledge described long ago by Piaget and Inhelder (1969) using terms which included equilibrium, disequilibrium, assimilation, and accommodation. No doubt, these terms were a part of your teacher training program.

More recently, we began to use the word "constructivism" to describe how the learner actively creates (constructs) new understanding through interaction with the environment. We know this process of interaction may modify current beliefs or understanding. In Piagetian terms, each of us strives to attain harmony or equilibrium. Through the introduction of something new we are placed in the state of disequilibrium. When we attempt to change that state back to equilibrium, we assimilate (or attempt to make what is new fit what we already know) or accommodate (modify our knowledge to fit the new information). As the two functions take place, we learn. Blais (1988) describes it in this way, "Knowledge is something that the learner must construct for himself. There is no alternative. Discovery, reinvention, or active reconstruction is necessary" (p. 3).

Therefore, in more simple terms, we can clearly see how some school practices such as the memorization of vocabulary definitions do not equal learning and they do not represent knowledge. Douglas (1989) stresses that what does matter in learning is "personal experiences" via active involvement. It is the "doing" of hands-on involvement we must offer children to ensure that they construct real knowledge. It may be in the form of reading, listening, painting, acting, creating, using, discussing, arguing, drawing, singing, and writing or any number of other "ings" that give teachers reason to believe real learning is taking place.

Another belief held by constructivists is that we don't all learn the same thing from the same experience. Each of our learning experiences is dependent on our prior knowledge and experiences. Therefore, the child who has visited the beach in South Carolina will better understand a story about the tides than the child who has not been to the ocean. Interests and past experiences play key roles in our level of understanding.

Louise Rosenblatt (1978, 1982) reminds us of this in terms of the books we read when she suggests that not all children who read a particular literature selection will take the same message from it. Rosenblatt uses the analogy of a musical performance. Although each performer may be reading the same piece of music with exactly the same notes, individual interpretations will be quite different and no two musicians will play it in quite the same way. Equally different is our interpretation of the written word.

You may have as many different opinions about the book, the actions of the characters, or the message the reader gets from the book as you do readers. Using literature does not, therefore, lend itself to right and wrong answers but to more interpretative kinds of thinking. Rosenblatt further applies this theory as she reminds us that reading is an active process in which literature serves as a means of personal exploration.

According to Rosenblatt, readers make choices to focus their attention in different ways during the process of reading. This is called the readers stance, and it does affect the way in which the reader addresses the text. Rosenblatt uses the terms *efferent* and *aesthetic* to describe the stance or approach the reader takes.

In taking the efferent stance, the reader focuses on gathering information. The reader pays special attention to what must be brought away from the passage. All of us use the efferent stance as we read new information about volcanoes, directions to the zoo, or how to program the VCR. We can see students taking an efferent stance in many book reports teachers assign. For instance, Robbie, a fourth grade student, recently read Spinelli's (1990) *Maniac Magee*. This is an excerpt from the oral book report he presented to his class.

> The Title: The book I read was *Maniac Magee*. It was written by Jerry Spinelli.
>
> The Main Characters: Maniac Magee is the main character. His real name is Jeffrey Lionel Magee. He comes to live in Two Mills when his parents die. He lives with the Beale family.
>
> Other Important Characters: Some other characters are Amanda Beale, Mars Bars, and Grayson.

The Setting: This story takes place in a town called Two Mills, Pennsylvania.

The Plot: In the book *Maniac Magee*, a boy named Jeffrey Lionel Magee, better known as Maniac Magee, comes to live in a town called Two Mills after his parents get killed in a car accident. He lives in lots of different places like with the Beale's and with Grayson, but he really wanted a real home with people who loved him. He became a hero in the story and did a lot of good for the town. He helped a lot of people who never got along get along better because of him.

My Opinion About the Book: This book was pretty good. It had lots of action and adventure. I liked the characters, especially Maniac, Grayson, and Mars Bars. I thought some of the characters seemed unreal and I didn't like that. A kid couldn't really move to another town by himself when his parents die and just live with other people. That seemed weird. One thing I did like was how the book was about a kid who likes to run. I like to run too and I want to be on the track team when I get into junior and senior high.

In Robbie's book report, we can see that he analyzed the content and included all the "parts" of a book report as the assignment required. In doing this, Robbie took the efferent stance—he read for information. Many teachers frame the assignment in this way to ensure that students have read the book. Missing or incorrect information would indicate that something was wrong. But, for those of us who have read Spinelli's book, we know there is so much more to this piece of literature. Maniac is a hero of sorts. He does it all—he beats Mars Bar running backwards, teaches the elder Grayson to read, gets the McNabb twins ready to go to school, but more important is that he brings a town that stood divided together again. He searches for a home throughout this entire story. Although he lives in many places, it is not until the end when Amanda Beale comes to the zoo and finds him that he realizes that someone is calling him "home." It's a wonderful story about needing to belong, about making change, and the power of love. However, when children only read to do a "fill in the blanks" book report or answer workbook questions, they run the risk of never really experiencing the story.

In the aesthetic stance, the reader attends to the feelings evoked and responses created during the reading. What did the book arouse or stir in the reader? As readers incorporate this stance, they draw on past experiences, consider relationships with other things, ponder the author's words and reasons for those words, and become more involved in the story. The reader "lives" through the reading of the story as did Jared, a child in another fourth grade class where the teacher encouraged his students to consider how they felt as they read the book. This is an excerpt from Jared's book report.

> My favorite thing about the book *Maniac Magee* is that Maniac was such a friend for Grayson. They both gave each other so much. As I read, I felt like I knew them. I kept thinking that if Grayson could find a different home and a better life it would be great! I wished Grayson could have been my friend. When I read this book, I thought of my grandfather. He's really not like Grayson, but I kept thinking that I hope he knows how we all love him and that he'll never be alone even when he is really old. How can people let old people be alone like that? I really loved reading this book. There were times when I felt really sad.

This skillful teacher had previously orchestrated discussions in his classroom that focused on the aesthetic stance. He also constructed the assignment in such a way that students were encouraged to "tell their own feelings" about the piece they had read. This can only happen if we as teachers guide our students to be more thoughtful, to be critical thinkers, and to make personal connections with the books they read.

These two ways of reading and reflecting on what we read can work together. It is important that teachers strive to use books in such a way to elicit both the efferent and aesthetic responses—there is a place for both kinds of reading. As classroom teachers, this may necessitate changing our teaching style and relinquishing our role as "all knowing teller of information" as we gravitate toward being more of a facilitator or orchestrator. In this role, we talk less and encourage our students to share more of themselves. We guide and direct and actually may find that saying less is really doing more in a different way. We can do this orchestration through the questions we ask, the assignments we give, the way we teach, and the encouragement we offer our students to share their ideas. Rosenblatt (1982) states that "the teacher's primary responsibility is to encourage the aesthetic stance" (p. 275).

We recognize that although both kinds of responses are appropriate, the efferent response is primarily encouraged by traditional basal series and skills instruction. Thus the focus is on story content and information rather than the reading experience itself. On the other hand, teachers who are more literature-based and support the underpinnings of a whole language philosophy are more apt to encourage their students to respond aesthetically. They encourage students to "see" the story in their minds ("I could really feel how much Matt loved the dog even if he didn't say it with words."); to hypothesize about what will happen ("As soon as they started talking about dying, I really knew someone would die in this story. I just couldn't figure out who."); to connect the story to other stories they know ("When I read this I thought of that story *Two Bad Ants,* because the pictures in this book are sort of like the pictures in that book, where you see things like you are the small ant."). The way in which you structure your teaching can incorporate a balance of both of these ways of reading and knowing.

What is Reading Competence?

Based on my own classroom practices as an elementary teacher, I vividly recall talking about reading development and competence in terms of vocabulary, comprehension, and oral fluency and expression during many parent conferences. It was the natural and expected way to view the reading process. Any reading teacher would be concerned with the recognition and understanding of words, the ability to extract meaning from text, and the smooth and expressive articulation of words.

During that part of my teaching career, I saw each of these elements of reading as separate competencies. Perhaps you see them that way as well. I made recommendations to parents about things they could do at home to strengthen their child's vocabulary, build comprehension, and develop better fluency and expression. Today, I have a very different view.

Rather than individual components that make up the mastery of reading, I see these as an interrelated set of competencies that develop together quite naturally. I concur with Frank Smith (1988) who reminds us that word meaning is dependent upon context—how the word is used in the sentence. I do not underestimate the effect one of these components has on the other, because I see them as clearly interwoven elements of the reading process. The more words the reader comes to understand the better his comprehension, fluency, and expression will be. As described by Vacca, Vacca, and Gove (1995)" . . . reading with expression is a sign of progress, a sign that a child is reading fluently and with comprehension" (p. 311).

As children read, they build on what they know and actively construct new understanding about the world around them (Goodman, 1972; Goodman and Goodman, 1977). Goodman's psycholinguistic model (which supports the constructivist theory of how readers achieve competence) has led to significant changes in the teaching of reading. This theory describes reading in terms of thought ("psycho") and language ("linguistics"). Readers are actively attempting to construct new meaning by combining their knowledge of language (i.e., speaking, listening, writing, and reading) with the knowledge of one's world (derived from daily experiences and background knowledge).

Quite simply, as a constructivist who aspires to the psycholinguistic model of reading, I support the notion that to help children become competent readers, we must offer an instructional program that includes frequent and ongoing opportunities to read, followed by many occasions to engage in challenging related experiences to expand their knowledge, use their skills, and offer engagement in active learning. All of this can best be accomplished within the literature-rich environment described in chapter 2.

The Constructivist Theory and Reading Instruction

Teachers who are themselves students of and believers in the constructivist theory, support the premise that children must be active learners. Therefore, children learn to read in much the same way children learn to use language. Parents do not "teach" their children the fundamentals of language by drilling them on words. A parent does not hold the fifteen month old and repeat, in any planned way, the 20 or 30 words many children that age have acquired as a part of their speaking vocabulary.

Rather, young children are immersed in language simply through their environments. They are spoken to and attempt to model what is heard. These approximations are often quite different from the words they are intended to be, but patient parents know that soon everyone will understand that "duh-duh-duh" means doggie! Through their immersion in a language-rich environment, rather than through planned and structured language "lessons" teaching individual sounds and the combining of those sounds to make words, children learn to speak and effectively master language. Reading is learned in much the same way.

Just as language skills are developed and perfected through experimentation with and use of speech as children attempt to communicate their wants, needs, and ideas (Dale, 1976; Jalongo, 1992), children improve in their reading proficiency with plenty of experimentation and error along the path to reading competence. In other words, we learn to read as we learn to talk, not through directed and fragmented lessons but through active participation, experimentation, and guided immersion in the process of developing proficiency and comprehension. Additional research (Wells, 1986; Taylor, 1983; Dyson, 1983, 1988) points toward the simultaneous development of speaking, writing, and reading and the obvious benefits in offering children opportunities to explore these areas in interrelated ways.

Today, many teachers are more in tune with experimentation as a part of the process of literacy development. They see errors as a natural prerequisite for growth and proficiency, and invented spelling is more understood and accepted. However, it is unfortunate that some teachers are still locked into the routine use of workbooks and black line masters that often squelch students' creativity. How unfortunate to see children who should be getting "hooked on books" and reveling in the countless opportunities to learn by doing, but who are instead feeling the pressure of right and wrong answers and the timely completion of workbook pages.

When I visit a classroom where this is the norm, I ask myself two questions. First, "What are the students actually learning about reading as they circle the correct answer or color the circle to mark the definition?" and "Shouldn't reading be more than this?" Think about these two questions as you plan your next reading lesson. How would you honestly answer them, and what might you do to improve student learning in your classroom?

What We Can Learn From Children

Recently, I asked, Tyler, a fourth grade friend of mine about his reading class. It was a simple and straightforward question, "What did you do in reading today?" He didn't hesitate to say, "We didn't have reading today." Each day for the next three days I asked the same question and got the same response. Finally, on day five, I was too curious to accept that answer, and I asked a few more questions about his time spent in school. My questions prompted Tyler to began talking enthusiastically about a book the class had been reading and discussing that entire week. It was *Hatchet* by Gary Paulsen.

Tyler said, "The book is so cool. We really like it and we are getting ready to do this group project about survival in the wilderness. It's really gonna be fun." I was shocked. This was the boy who each day told me that he had not had reading class and now he was excitedly telling me about the week's reading! Where had we miscommunicated?

Finally, I asked, "Tyler, I thought you told me you didn't have reading at all this week?" "Oh we didn't, " he said. "We didn't use the reading books and workbooks all week and boy this is a whole lot better!"

I was both sad and glad. Sad that this ten-year-old saw reading as merely a subject in school where you use the reading book and workbook. I was deeply concerned about his narrow view and misconceptions about reading. It made me wonder how many other children envision reading in that same way. This scenario also made me glad— delighted that he was so enthralled and excited about Gary Paulsen's wonderful adventure story and that he was greatly anticipating the future class activities.

Teachers can learn a great deal from Tyler's perceptions of reading. We do children a disservice by allowing the word "reading" to be so narrowly defined. We must find a way to show our young readers that reading is so much more than only what takes place in reading class. We can and do read in all content areas, and we read in all kinds of daily situations. Through our personal daily examples and our teaching, children should see and understand that reading is more than a class—it is getting information and enjoyment from the printed word and undoubtedly can take many forms, from the efferent reading of the newspaper or repair manual, to the aesthetic reading of a book, that gives us reason to consider how our lives may be like that of the character we have come to know and understand.

What Exactly Does This Mean for Me?

Perhaps you are a bit puzzled, wondering how all of this will impact your teaching in general and, specifically, your delivery of reading instruction. Maybe you are thinking something similar to what Deanna, a second grade teacher, said "This all makes perfect sense to me, but the picture I see in my mind as I read about all of this constructivist theory and aesthetic stance doesn't exactly describe what you would see in my classroom." Marion, a teacher with 22 years in first grade, expresses similar sentiments with, "This is not how I was trained to teach. I feel at a real loss." Lynn, a third grade teacher asks, "But, where is the real teaching of reading?" All of these are valid and expected questions from teachers who are wrestling with making change.

Each of us is familiar with "our way" of teaching reading. You know how you or your school district has designed the reading program and how you have applied this design to your classroom practice. This book is not written to criticize certain practices and celebrate others. Rather, it is written to describe what is currently known about how children learn, how they become literate, and how they perfect their reading competence. It has also been written to offer a variety of instructional strategies to help teachers on their journey to create proficient readers and to inspire more positive attitudes toward reading.

You, the reader, are encouraged to consider the research, the teacher vignettes and anecdotes, and instructional ideas this book offers and to identify ways in which to expand or modify your repertoire. Through your self-examination and reflection, you may see new strategies, instructional designs, and techniques you would like to implement in your classroom. Maybe you see a little change in order or perhaps a considerable transformation in your teaching of reading. Let's begin with looking at beliefs about reading.

Beliefs About Reading

It is how you believe a reader translates print into meaning that will help you identify the reading model with which your philosophical beliefs most closely align. Too often, teachers find themselves unhappily making changes in their reading instruction without a personal commitment and understanding. Perhaps it is your school district's new commitment to whole language that is gently (or not so gently) pushing you to attend workshops, teach with literature, change teaching strategies, implement new grouping practices, and revise district curriculum—all in one year! You may find yourself going through the motions and complying with rapid change with little time for consideration and thoughtful reflection about your own beliefs about reading and how they might translate into program implementation.

Your beliefs should drive your teaching. Each of us can benefit from careful consideration of our past experiences in teaching reading, the feedback (both spoken and implied) from our students, what we have learned from colleagues, and our own efforts in professional development to decide where we are on this issue. These beliefs will help us decide the role literature plays in our teaching and how we can best implement it into our classroom practices. Maybe a lot; maybe a little. But first let's get a little more personal.

In order to consider ways to improve your reading instruction, you must first recognize your own instructional beliefs about reading. You are encouraged to be reflective and consider what you see as the best practices for children. Once you can identify those, it will be easier to implement the new strategies you want to use in your classroom.

These personal beliefs which are based on our educational training, our practical daily experiences in the classroom, our interactions with and observations of students, our professional development activities, and our successes and failures over time form the basis of how we teach and work with our students. These beliefs are very fluid; as we grow and change, so do they. What we believed about learning and teaching during our first year of teaching no doubt changed considerably before the second, third, fifth, and tenth years. Hopefully, we will continue to consider our beliefs and be open to change as long as we teach. I encourage each of you to make a list that describes your personal feelings and beliefs about learning and teaching (see Figure 3.1). What helps children learn? What is your role as teacher in the learning process? What are some things you know to be true about children and the developmental processes they experience at school and at home? These tenets will serve as the foundation for building the use of literature in your classroom.

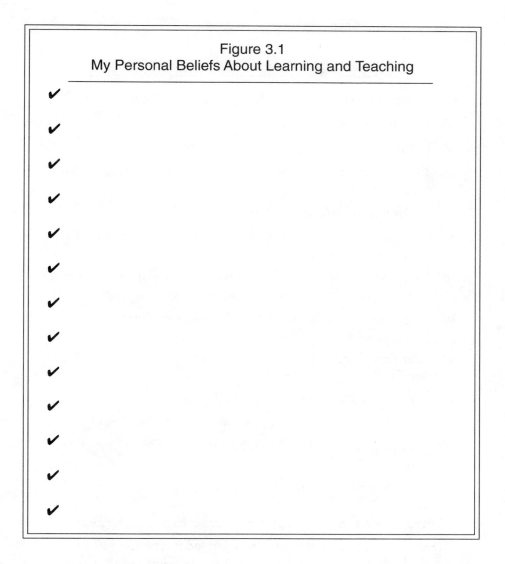

Figure 3.1
My Personal Beliefs About Learning and Teaching

In Figure 3.2, I have also identified some of the components and beliefs I consider essential and true about learning and teaching. These have evolved over my teaching career and are certainly not the same set of beliefs I might have written five or ten years ago (although some of my beliefs have remained constant). Over time and as a result of my experiences, I have made changes—some subtle and others more noticeable. I know they will continue to change in some way as I continue to learn. I share them merely as a way to move you toward thinking about your own beliefs. Similarly, what you have written in Figure 3.1 tells a great deal about your own work with children and the paths to learning and teaching you will follow.

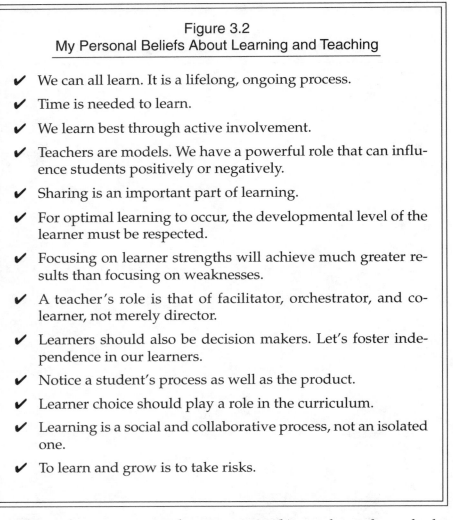

Figure 3.2
My Personal Beliefs About Learning and Teaching

✔ We can all learn. It is a lifelong, ongoing process.

✔ Time is needed to learn.

✔ We learn best through active involvement.

✔ Teachers are models. We have a powerful role that can influence students positively or negatively.

✔ Sharing is an important part of learning.

✔ For optimal learning to occur, the developmental level of the learner must be respected.

✔ Focusing on learner strengths will achieve much greater results than focusing on weaknesses.

✔ A teacher's role is that of facilitator, orchestrator, and co-learner, not merely director.

✔ Learners should also be decision makers. Let's foster independence in our learners.

✔ Notice a student's process as well as the product.

✔ Learner choice should play a role in the curriculum.

✔ Learning is a social and collaborative process, not an isolated one.

✔ To learn and grow is to take risks.

Although you may never have recognized it, you have always had a set of beliefs about teaching. Unfortunately, we don't often think about them and even less often do we articulate them. Take time to do this before you go on to chapter 4.

References

Blais, D. (1988). Constructivism: A theoretical revolution in teaching. *Journal of Developmental Education, 11*(3), 2–7.

Dale, P. (1976). *Language development*. New York: Hold, Rinehart, and Winston.

Douglas, M. P. (1989). *Learning to read: The quest for meaning*. New York: Teachers College Press.

Dyson, A. H. (1983). The role of oral language in early writing processes. *Research in the Teaching of English, 17,* 1–30.

Dyson, A. H. (1988). Negotiating among multiple worlds: The space/time dimensions of young children's composing. *Research in the Teaching of English, 22,* 355–390.

Goodman, K. S. (1972). *The reading process: Theory and practice.* In R. E. Hodges & E. H. Rudorf (Eds.), *Language and learning to read* (pp. 143–159). Boston: Houghton Mifflin.

Goodman, K. S. & Goodman, Y. M. (1977). Learning about psycholinguistic processes by analyzing oral reading. *Harvard Educational Review, 47,* 317–333.

Jalongo, M. R. (1992). *Early childhood language arts.* Needham Heights, MA: Allyn and Bacon.

Piaget, J. and Inhelder, B. (1969). *The psychology of the child.* (H. Weaver, trans.) New York: Basic Books.

Rosenblatt, L. (1978). *The reader, the text, the poem: The transactional theory of the literary work.* Carbondale, IL: Southern Illinois University Press.

Rosenblatt, L. (1982). The literary transaction: Evocation and response. *Theory into Practice, 21,* 268–277.

Smith, F. (1988). *Joining the literacy club: Further essays into education.* Portsmouth, NH: Heinemann.

Taylor, D. (1983). *Family literacy: Young children learning to read and write.* Portsmouth, NH: Heinemann.

Vacca, J., Vacca, R. T., & Gove, M. K. (1995). *Reading and learning to read* (3rd Ed.). New York: HarperCollins.

Wells, G. (1986). *The meaning makers: Children learning language and using language to learn.* Portsmouth, NH: Heinemann.

Children's Books

Paulsen, G. (1987). *Hatchet.* New York: Bradbury.

Spinelli, J. (1990). *Maniac Magee.* New York: Little, Brown & Company.

Stewart, S. (1995). *The library.* New York: Farrar, Straus & Giroux.

Van Allsburg, C. (1988). *Two bad ants.* New York: Houghton Mifflin.

Part 3

The Reality of Using Literature

One of the biggest problems teachers face in the incorporation of literature into their reading program and classroom teaching is being unsure of "just how do I make it happen." Part 3 examines this very important mission.

Chapter 4, "Incorporating Literature into the Classroom," examines how teachers begin making the transition to bolster the use of literature in their teaching. As one teacher portrayed it, "It really is more that just reading books to students." This chapter will help you examine the three major reading theories and the beliefs they offer.

Chapter 4 also offers a number of organizational frameworks for designing a program to integrate literature into your existing classroom structure. The "personal design" of a reading program makes it possible for teachers to weave literature into existing reading programs even if you are "locked into" a commercial reading series.

Another feature of this chapter that teachers will find especially helpful are the numerous comments from teachers who are "making it happen."

Chapter 5, "Choosing Appropriate Books and Activities," will not attempt to tell you the best books to read or the most appropriate activities to use. Rather, this chapter will attempt to give you the tools and guidance you need to select the books which are best for your audience. By understanding what to look for in the selection of quality books, you will have the skill to choose books for any age or group of children.

4

Incorporating Literature into the Classroom

Alice was beginning to get very tired of sitting by her sister on the bank, and of having nothing to do; once or twice she had peeped into the book her sister was reading, but it had no pictures or conversations in it, "and what is the use of a book," thought Alice, "without pictures or conversation?"

Lewis Carroll, 1963, p. 1

Alice was right. Pictures and conversation do make books more "real," just as the glimpses of classrooms and the comments of teachers found in this chapter will help us better understand some of what we want to accomplish in our own classrooms. They make it all seem more tangible and achievable. However, let me caution you that this is not something for which there is a recipe or prescription. It involves more than the cookbook approach that says, "first you do this, and then you do this, and so on." It is a continuous process, and what follows are some thoughts on that process to consider before the first real step is even taken.

Before You Begin

First you have to believe in yourself; the answers will come. You have to know what you really think about how children learn, how they become better readers, and what needs to happen to excite children about reading so that they will become life-long readers. We must also realize that there are no right or wrong ways to becoming the best reading teachers we can be. You must do what you are comfortable doing. You must do what meets your needs and the needs of your children. You must do what is in line with what your school district will support.

Before teachers begin this journey of change, they must know that mistakes are a part of the journey. You must read, think, try, and reflect. What would I do differently next time? What went (perhaps surprisingly) well and which aspects of what I attempted would I do again? Be both a knowledgeable and reflective practitioner.

Realize that you might have to make a transition in your way of working with children that calls for you to give up some control. You may need to move from being that always in charge kind of teacher, who knows exactly how it should go, to being more flexible and open to try new things. Remember, there may be times that both you and your students will be learners. Becoming the facilitator rather than the director may also mean reducing control over the materials you use. You may, however, find yourself taking more responsibility for the materials you use and the way in which you use them. You may find yourself deciding what and how you teach, rather than allowing the book companies and commercial programs to control your instruction.

Before you begin, you must recognize that what works for you may not work for your fellow teachers. Our thoughts about teaching reading may be very personal and individual. Some of us have more freedom and flexibility given to us than others. We must work within the constraints we have.

The basal reader does not need to be condemned and thrown aside. The materials do not make the teacher; the teacher and his or her beliefs about teaching and learning make the teacher. You can be locked into using a commercially produced series and not encouraged to use literature, but you can still make learning to read more active and engaging by implementing some of the tenets explored in this book. Teaching the basal does not negate opportunities to infuse quality literature into your reading program.

Recognize, too, that you will need to start small and build. It is a process that takes time and should not be attempted in one large leap. Time, patience, and small steps will all add to your level of success.

What Do I Do First?

Now that you have articulated those beliefs that direct your teaching, it is time to make a plan. What are your realistic goals? What would you like to change? Achieve? Add to your program? Eliminate? If I decide to supplement or eliminate the basal as my primary form of instruction, what organizational strategies are available to me? Let's briefly examine the three basic theories of reading to see where we are and where we would like to go.

What Does Reading Theory Say?

Reading models have been developed to help us define the way in which the reader constructs meaning from print. There are three primary models of the reading process which have been widely used in education during the last forty years. Some of the significant names associated with these theories are Jeanne Chall (1967, 1985), Rudolph Flesch (1956), Ken Goodman (1986, 1996), Frank Smith (1979), Regie Routman (1988, 2000), and Keith Stanovich (1986). Some of these may be familiar to you; but more important than their names are their ideas. Which model do you most closely associate with?

Bottom-Up Model

In this model of reading, the process of translating print to meaning begins with the print and the decoding of graphic symbols into sound. First, students begin with the recognition of the graphic symbols we call letters, and then learn to decode the symbols into sounds. The child then combines letters and their sounds to recognize spelling and sound patterns. He then puts together sounds to recognize words, and continues on with this building process to recognize and read sentences, paragraphs, and so on. The process of deriving meaning is dependent upon the reader's ability to rapidly process graphophonic information. Therefore, students become readers through the mastery of word recognition skills. Readers comprehend what they read through their ability to unlock unfamiliar words. It is a theory driven by a skills-based curriculum typically found in basal reading programs. Evaluation in this model primarily focuses on the more formal and traditional methods provided by workbooks and worksheets.

Top-Down Model

The top-down model emphasizes that the reader's processing of information (comprehension) is not triggered by word recognition alone, but is greatly supported by a individual's prior knowledge and experience. A proponent of this model, Frank Smith (1979) states, "The more you already know, the less you need to find out" (p. 15). What he means by this is that readers are less dependent upon word sound associations (graphophonemic information) because of their prior knowledge of the topic. The reader makes predictions and educated guesses about the meaning of some print and uses what he knows about the different conventions of capital letters, grammar, context, and semantics, as well as graphophonic information, to gain meaning.

In the Top-Down Model, meaning and word recognition can be arrived at through a variety of cues rather than the sole use of letter-sound associations. Reading for meaning is stressed and students are engaged in meaningful activities that include all the language modalities of reading, writing, listening, and speaking. Evaluation procedures include portfolios, running records, reading inventories, interviews, and kidwatching with anecdotal notes. All of which allow the teacher to gather useful information about student performance.

Interactive Model of Reading

Many recognize this as a more balanced approach since the reader uses both prior knowledge and graphophonic information. The process offers a "blend" and is initiated by making predictions about meaning and decoding the graphic symbols. Phonics is taught not in isolation, but in a print-rich context. Most often, those who align themselves with this approach will use a literature-based program to achieve their goals. A summary of the three models of reading instruction can be found in Figure 4.1.

Figure 4.1 Beliefs About Reading			
	Bottom–Up	**Top–Down**	**Interactive**
How Word Recognition Aids Comprehension	To comprehend, students must recognize each word. Phonics is stressed.	Comprehension can be achieved even when students cannot recognize each word. The reader makes meaning using knowledge and experience.	Comprehension is achieved through graphophonic information and prior knowledge.
Using Cues in Reading	Sound-letter cues are used to recognize unfamiliar words.	Context, grammatical, graphic, and meaning cues help to recognize unfamiliar words.	Word decoding supported by context and meaning cues to help form hypotheses and gather meaning.
Important Components	Recognizing words is stressed.	Reading for meaning is stressed.	A balance of both bottom-up and top-down components is for reading success.
Philosophical Tenets	Students become readers through the mastery and use of word recognition skills.	Students become readers through meaningful activities in which they read, write, speak, and listen.	Students become readers through making meaning (comprehending) through interaction with print.
			cont.

Curriculum	Driven by skills-based curriculum focusing on basal reading programs	Driven by a more whole language curriculum using authentic texts.	Utilizes a balanced approach usually teaching phonics within a print-rich literature-based program.
Thoughts on Assessment	Students are evaluated on individual skills through the use of workbooks and other paper-pencil graded tasks.	Students are evaluated in a variety of more informal ways to assess the kind of knowledge constructed through reading.	Students are evaluated through a combination of formal and informal measures for a clear picture of individual growth.

Through which "lens" do you view the process of reading? Give it careful consideration so that you are ready to proceed to the next step of designing an organizational framework for your own classroom. Your design should be a blend of what you believe about reading and what you found to be your "match" in reading models.

Incorporating an Organizational Framework

Now that you have considered what you hope to achieve to compliment your personal belief system and your school's philosophical stance, and you have given thought to the three reading models, you are ready to think about classroom organizational patterns. This is where you will answer the question, "How will I put my beliefs into practice?"

In order to help you make those plans, this chapter will discuss organizational frameworks seen in many reading classrooms. Consider each of them and what they offer you and your students. How can one or many of these work in your classroom? What changes might be needed for your organizational patterns to become reality?

As you read about each, please keep in mind that there are numerous possible combinations of patterns. Different teachers will use these methods of organizing instruction in different ways, incorporating different degrees of involvement. It is also important to remember that some teachers are using these methods in tandem with their basal programs.

Core Books

Sometimes teachers will organize their classroom instruction around a predetermined list of core books designated for their grade level. School districts will encourage teachers to work together on curriculum committees to select trade books for each grade. Criteria considered in this process include readability and connections with existing curriculum. This is often done in schools where teachers desire to move away from the basal reading program.

Once the core book lists are completed, teachers work together to design curriculum guides. These often include everything one needs to know (the proverbial soup to nuts approach) including a summary of the book, information about the author, information about each character, new vocabulary words, questions to ask the reader, reading skills to be taught, and extension activities integrating the book into other curriculum areas.

Some may find this approach a very inclusive and complete way to use literature, while others may see disadvantages to this organizational plan. Those who are less than enthusiastic about the use of core books often describe this as the "basalizing" of literature and consider just what teachers should be attempting to reduce and/or eliminate. Basalization often results in students completing worksheets, responding to literal comprehension questions, and engaging in round-robin reading (Zarillo, 1989). Although core books can be poorly used, there certainly are ways to use core books to provide quality literary experiences in your classroom.

Core books can be quite effective if we recall our earlier discussion of reading stance. Children should be encouraged to take both an efferent and aesthetic stance to their reading. In other words, we need to develop questions which encourage both convergent ("What did Sam want for his birthday?") and divergent thinking ("If you had been Sam, what might you have chosen for your birthday and why?").

When a reader takes an aesthetic stance, encouraged by the questions the teacher asks and the assignments the teacher designs, we hear students responding about how the text made them feel and how it connected to their own experiences.

Many teachers find core books useful as a part of the reading program rather than the entire reading program. Experiment and see what works best for you. Perhaps you will find that using the core book approach works best when flanked with a literature unit, self-selected reading, and even basal instruction!

Make Excellent Book Choices: Select core books you like and you know will be enjoyed by your students. They should be books you will love being engaged with over time since the use of a particular core book can typically extend from a few days to several weeks in the upper grades. We need to recognize that not all books are excellent ones, and it is important to preview each book on the list before deciding on one. If you feel very positively about the value of the book and all it has to offer your students, it will be evident in your enthusiasm for reading the book. The excitement for the book begins with the teacher and is contagious!

Make the Presentation of the Book Memorable: Remember the mention of the "parsley on the plate" in chapter 1? As teachers of reading, we need to present the books we select with enthusiasm, excitement, emotion, and drama! Whether we are reading parts aloud or building the excitement for the next chapter with the development of a gripping anticipatory set, one of our goals should be to have our audience clamoring for more! In the classrooms of our youngest reader/listeners we hear the words, "Read it again," shouted out from the children. With the older children, the excitement is similarly demonstrated as Derek, a boy who typically struggles with reading books, raised his hand to say, "Please read just one more chapter before lunch. You can't stop there!" It is our responsibility as teachers of reading to present a book in the most dramatic and exciting way possible.

Independent Reading and Writing: Remember that flexibility we discussed in an earlier chapter? Hang on to your hats—here is comes. Recently, I visited a third grade classroom where the children were using the book, *Sarah, Plain and Tall* (MacLachlan, 1985) as one of their core books. When I arrived, the children were all reading independently at various places around the room. The teacher had apparently asked that they not go beyond a certain point in their reading. Jennifer, however, had really been engrossed in her reading, and when the teacher realized that she was two chapters beyond where she was to be, there was quite uproar on the part of the teacher. So much for the notion of student interest!

I was surprised to see that this teacher displayed such inflexibility in the matter. Jennifer defended her actions with a simple, "It was getting so good, Mrs. Pentall, I couldn't put it down." To me that was a great testimonial about a great book; but to this teacher, it was a grave error on the student's part.

I've tried to look at this situation from everyone's perspective, but I'm not sure that this "reading ahead" was as serious as Mrs. Pentall thought. I would have been delighted that any child in my class was so excited about reading a book. Part of what we as teachers aspire to do is as O'Malley (1997) says, ". . . fan the flame to extend the experience of learning and reading" (p. 5). It appears that the flame had been sufficiently fanned. The interest was there, and I would suspect that the possibility of Jennifer wanting to read another book about this period in history such as *Caddie Woodlawn* (Brink, 1970) or *Little House in the Big Woods* (Wilder, 1953) when she had finished the core book would have been readily accepted. Why must everyone always read exactly the same thing at the very same time? Certainly there are times when this is most appropriate, but as teachers hoping to encourage interest in reading, we should remember that children need opportunities to read independently when they are so moved.

Not only should we be encouraging interest in reading, but also interest in writing. Be cautious of publishing companies which produce booklets of dittoed-nonsense and keep-them-busy-worksheets. Guides such as these can turn literature into a boring teaching tool and make children appreciate books less rather than more. Recently, I visited a fifth grade classroom reading Taylor's wonderful book, *Roll of Thunder, Hear My Cry* (1976). Although not a book appropriate for the grades we are focusing on in this book, the point I want to make holds true for all grades. The children had just read the first 12 pages of the book and were asked to get out their "booklets." I wondered what these booklets would be. I was very disappointed.

Each child had a fifteen-page set of reproduced worksheets about the book. The tasks ranged from vocabulary words that needed to be looked up in the dictionary and a definition written, to questions (all very low level) such as "List the names of the children and their ages." So much for character development, making connections with our own life experiences, testing hypotheses, and sharing feelings about the events in the book. It was a shameful basalization of a wonderfully powerful and meaningful book.

Why couldn't the children have created character webs; written letters to the stories main character, Cassie, comparing their school with the school she attended; or discussed in small groups those family possessions that might be as important as the land was to the Logan family? This easily could have happened if the teacher had considered how children learn and how we can excite children about the books we ask them to read.

 Activities as a follow up to core-books (such as those in chapter 6 that encourage active involvement) need to digress from skill-drill types of worksheets. They need to actively involve children in more authentic and meaningful tasks. Teachers, however, need to recognize that more is not better with activities. They are to be used in moderation, not excess. They do have a place in the use of literature, but the activities should not drive the use of the book, and plenty of time should be set aside for reading and writing. Many teachers have found success in designing a number of activities related to a particular core book and allowing children to select one or two that they will do during and after the reading.

Literature Units

Another way to organize instruction is around a literature unit model. Such units are linked by a unifying element which might include the author, the genre, the theme, the content, or the literary elements. Whatever element binds these books, the primary goal should be one of broadening the horizons of the students. In such a plan, the children usually have choices as to which books they will read and which activities they might pursue. Such units are a great way to introduce children to all kinds of books. For instance, if the theme was "Family," the teacher would bring a number of age and grade appropriate books about families to the classroom. These would represent fiction and non-fiction and might fall into the genres of poetry, realistic fiction, fantasy, and historical fiction. (If you had 24 children, I might suggest 30 plus titles to allow for easy selection and switching of books.) These books might each be a different title or you may use duplicate copies of certain books.

The main goal of a literature unit is to get children to read, so when a child finishes one book, there should be a sufficient supply of books to self-select another. Following the reading of a book, students will have opportunities to meet independently with the teacher and to also work in small groups. Responses from children are encouraged, and activities and projects maintain an important place in literature units.

Literature Circles

A literature circle is a way to engage children not only in the reading, but most importantly in conversations about what they read. In reading circles, several students who have read a certain literature selection form a small group where they share comments, questions, issues, and thoughts about what they have all read. Discussions develop about the book, the author, the theme, the characters, and so on. The teacher does not take an active role in the discussion, and the students are the directors of the conversations.

This is how Katie, a third grade teacher, used literature circles in her classroom. Katie used a variety of instructional strategies and organizational patterns. She believed the variety helped keep her reading instruction fresh and exciting. Here are her thoughts on how she engaged her students in independent learning through literature circles.

> I see literature circles as offering my students three important learning experiences. One, it offers children the opportunity of making choices about what they will read. Second, it

offers readers the chance to read independently and at their own pace. Third, it shows children how to work collaboratively as they support and learn from each other. I see the teacher as an important player, but not in the way I was most familiar with. It is a new role for both student and teacher. It was certainly a new role for me.

When I use literature circles I do it in this way: On Monday, I introduce the class to a number of books I have previously selected for use in literature circles. I do a brief book talk on each, trying to make each book equally exciting. I place each of the books (there are always multiple copies of most titles) in a large wicker clothesbasket. The students are instructed to select one book that sounds interesting to them and that they can anticipate reading by the end of the week. Teams are then formed based on book titles rather than ability grouping. I encourage teams of 3–5 members. If more wish to join a team, I help the group divide into 2 more teams.

Students read their books independently throughout the week. Since team members are reading the same book, they are encouraged to help each other when they encounter unfamiliar words or any other questions or confusion in their reading. However, I am always available, and I circulate the room interacting with group members, keeping readers on task, asking questions, and so on. By Friday, it is expected that all books will be read and the groups will come together to talk. This has taken more than a little planning and a lot of modeling to have it happen effectively. This is not the only way I teach reading, but it is one of the many pieces of my reading program.

Each year it takes several less-than-successful tries before literature circles look like literature circles and before I feel satisfied that they are where I want them to be. Most often, the students are so accustomed to teachers directing everything that they are a little timid about generating their own questions and discussions. Others are most comfortable being a "hitchhiker" in these kinds of activities. It takes a diligent teacher who doesn't give up on modeling and working toward the goals of literature circles. These goals include having each team member attending to the topic, participating actively, asking questions for clarification, piggybacking off others' comments, and learning to disagree constructively and in a positive way ("I don't agree with that, Jeff, because _____." rather than "You're wrong, Jeff!").

I recommend that teachers begin with whole group literature circles. Doing these as a sort of "practice literature circle" allows the class to feel more comfortable when we do literature circles with small groups without me there with them every minute. In this practice kind of circle, I can model how questions are asked and how the process works. Some teachers even encourage the students to begin offering questions for the group while the teacher is still present in the large 'practice' literature circle. In this way, the teacher's role begins to become more secondary and the students take ownership in the process. With practice and sufficient modeling, students become quite capable of choosing their questions and even deciding how much should be read before the next meeting. Sometimes, I will offer the students some ideas for discussion if I think they need that sort of prompt. After they do this a few times, they can really go with it and I find prompts to be unnecessary.

I had some doubt at first; but I'm really glad I stuck with it. I now value literature circles as a very effective part of my reading program.

Reading Workshops

The idea of reading workshops was originated by Nanci Atwell (1987) as a way to integrate literature and the language arts. In this framework to organize and manage your literacy-centered classroom, the entire class is engaged in reading, responding, and sharing books with the teacher and peers. Although it provides time for the teacher to help students, the heart of the reading workshop is reading.

It consists of five main components: teacher sharing time, mini lessons, status-of-the-class conference, self-selected reading and responding, and student sharing time.

Teacher Sharing Time: This is when the teacher "sets the stage" and motivates the students through the sharing of literature. Perhaps she will read Aileen Fisher's poem, "The Furry Ones" (1971) to warm up the class and excite them about the upcoming study of insects; or she read an excerpt from Lois Lowrey's (1995) *Anastasia, Absolutely* to prepare them for Calliope Day, a similar heroine they will soon meet in another book.

Mini Lessons: The teacher takes a few minutes after sharing time to demonstrate a brief lesson on a strategy or skill. This may be designed to meet a specific need demonstrated in a student conference, provide prereading support, background for reading, or vocabulary for a book students are about to read. Regardless of what the mini lesson includes, it should incorporate the skills or strategy within the context of a specific piece of literature they have already read or listened to or will be reading next. It may be done as a whole class or a small group. The focus is that this remain short (five to ten minutes) and be drawn from the observed needs of students rather than something that is prescribed in a teacher's manual.

Status-of-the-Class-Conference: This is a brief "look-see" time where the teacher takes stock of what the individual students are doing or planning to do during sustained silent reading time and/or group activity. It is recommended that the teacher keep a chart of each child's plan for the day. Figure 4.2 shows a simple yet very telling chart kept by one fourth grade teacher as she conducted reading workshops in her classroom. At first, many teachers prefer to handle the record keeping themselves. As the children become more comfortable with the organization of the reading workshop, a large chart may be posted each week and students can discuss their plans during this brief status-of-the-class conference time and commit themselves by entering their plans on the chart.

Sustained Silent Reading and Responding: During SSR everyone, including the classroom teacher, reads a self-selected book. This is free reading time, but all must participate. Typically it ranges from 15–60 minutes, depending upon the age of your students and the amount of time you have within your school day for all five parts of the reading workshop to take place. This should be the longest portion of the five workshop components.

SSR is the core of the reading workshop and students may read independently or with a partner. As you, the teacher and model, read, one eye should be on the students who might need additional motivation and encouragement. Students also have the responsibility of responding to the literature in some way following the completion of the reading. The response activity might include journal writing, working in a literature circle, or other activities dependent upon the creativity of the teacher and interest of the students. These activities should cover a number of language modalities including reading, writing, listening, and speaking. Some teachers have designed the responses to fit in certain categories such as artistic, written, dramatization, and oral. One teacher who had effectively done this reports that she requires her children to do one activity of each type before choosing a second activity in any one particular area. Many creative responses to literature are described in chapter 6.

Figure 4.2
Status-of-the-Class Chart

STATUS-OF-THE-CLASS

Name	M	T	W	Th	F

Key:
SSR - Self-selected reading   RK - Record Keeping
J   - Journal   G   - Goal Setting
R   - Response Activity   D   - Discussing
LC   - Literature Circle Meeting

Another student responsibility is to keep an up-to-date log of their reading choices and time spent in SSR. Students need to project when they will be ready for an individual conference with the teacher. Although the teacher is also reading silently during this time, when students are ready to conference, the teacher stops reading to conduct conferences. The teacher should not be writing lesson plans, checking papers, or hanging the new bulletin board. Doing so would send a powerful message that reading is not important to you. Be a model and an active participant in the reading workshop as you read yourself or participate in reading conferences and discussions.

Individual Reading Conferences: Each day the teacher will meet with several students who have indicated they are ready for a conference. Most teachers using this strategy have found it more successful when the teacher identifies time slots for conferences and students are responsible for making appointments on a sign up board at least one day in advance. Many teachers also build into the reading workshop plan a minimal number of conferences for each student during a given period of weeks or during a grading period. This is certainly best designed once you have determined the amount of time to be spent with reading workshops.

During the conference, the teacher and students discuss the book which has been read. Questions are posed by the teacher and should focus on higher-level thinking skills rather than the low-level, more literal questions discussed in earlier chapters. Teachers often express concern when they ask, "How can I keep one step ahead of the students so that I have read every book the students might choose?" It is a daunting task, but that need not interfere with your conference and questioning. Teachers can easily design more generic kinds of questions that would be applicable for any book a child might read. Some examples might include:

- What did you find particularly funny? Interesting? Thrilling? Unusual? And why?
- Has anything you read about in this book ever happened to you? Tell about it.
- Do you see yourself as being like any of the characters in the book? Who and what are the similarities?
- From reading the story, do you think there is a message here for the reader? If so, what?

A list of additional sample questions that can fit almost any book your students might choose can be found in Figure 4.3.

Individual conferences usually last from 5–8 minutes and can give both teacher and student an opportunity to not only more fully understand and appreciate the story, as well as getting to know each other a little better.

Figure 4.3. Good Questions Get Readers Thinking

1. What has happened in the story that has also happened to you?

2. Is your life at all like any character in the book? How?

3. Have you known people like those in the book? Who and how are they alike?

4. What things happened in the book that you would like to have happen to yourself? Why?

5. What did a character do that you also could do?

6. What did a character do that you would not/could not do?

7. What did a character do that you would like to do?

8. What did a character do that you are afraid to do?

9. Why did this book make you feel good/bad/nothing? Tell about it.

10. How would you have changed this story?

11. What can you guess about the characters that is not told about them?

12. Is there another book you have listened to or read like this one? How is it similar?

13. Was there anything in the book you couldn't understand?

14. What happened in the book that angered, disturbed, or startled you?

15. What was the author doing to make you laugh?

16. Was the book happy or gloomy? Why?

17. Did the book move fast or slowly? Why do you say that?

18. What kind of experiences do you think the author needed to have to write this book?

19. If you helped someone get ready to read this book, what would you say?

20. Can you find many unusual words that the author used?

21. How did you learn what each character in the book was like? Explain.

22. Is the place in which this story happens like any place you know?

23. Is there a hero/heroine in the story? Who and why?

Sharing Time: During the last 5-10 minutes of the reading workshop, the students come together to share their books and activities. It may be to show a finished project or a work in progress. Simply ask your students "Where are you at this point in time and how have you spent the last ____ minutes?"

Student sharing time is a wonderful way to spread the excitement toward books. You may find it more manageable to divide the class into several smaller groups or to have a longer sharing time based on the number of projects to be shared. This sharing time is an invaluable part of the reading process. Please always find a way to allow students to share their responses to literature.

Tips from Practicing Teachers

Many teachers use literature in their classrooms every day. For each of them, the journey has been different. What follows are some of their stories, suggestions, successes, and failures. They hope their journeys will help, support and energize you as you implement literature into your classroom practices.

Nancy—First Grade Teacher

Resources, or the lack of them, certainly play a big part in using literature in the classroom. This initially was a big problem for me. Since then, I have really used my school library to access quality literature; and I recommend that all teachers make friends with your school librarian. They know what is there and they can help you out. I have also written a few small grants which paid for books for my classroom, but I realize that this may not be an option for every teacher. However, book clubs like Scholastic, Troll, Trumpet, and Carnival are available to all teachers

When I began teaching, I used a lot of books from my own childhood collection and started making the book clubs available to my students. Through their book purchases I was able to collect a number of bonus points which helped me build my classroom library. When this is done in conjunction with other teachers at your grade level you can develop quite a collection of books.

Don't be afraid to ask your administrators if they are willing to set aside a few hundred dollars each year toward the purchase of trade books. Keep in mind that every workbook and practice book from the commercial reading program costs between $7.00 and $12.00. By cutting back on these purchases, money can be channeled toward building your book collection.

Also remember that both small neighborhood bookstores as well as the larger chains have discounts for teachers. I've just received an "educators card" that entitles me to a 20 percent discount at the three major chains in my area: Borders, Waldenbooks, and Barnes and Noble. Teachers need to be good consumers and shop where the buys are!

One last way to acquire the books you need for your reading program might come from one of the most overlooked sources—parents. Each year the children in my class were coming up with more and more elaborate birthday celebrations with treats, favors, and party games. It was getting to be too much, so I recommended that parents keep the birthday simple and contribute, instead, a book or two to our classroom library. I have a list of recommended titles for parents who are interested. At the birthday celebration we introduce the new book and insert a bookplate in the book for all the children to see. I think that the way in which this is handled lets children know that books and reading are very important in our classroom.

Barb—A Second Grade Teacher

I have made significant changes in my teaching from using the traditional basal program to a more literature based approach. I can remember asking myself some of the same questions I suppose many teachers worry about like, "How can I get away from the traditional two reading groups?" First, I started reading more. I began about ten years ago by reading The Reading Teacher regularly. At that time, they seemed to have a lot of articles about journaling with students. In addition to reading The Reading Teacher, I came across Regie Routman's first book, Transitions. Finding that was wonderful. She was about my age at the time and had been trained as a traditional basal teacher. It seemed she was telling my story and writing from my perspective. She was writing as someone who also wanted to make this change. She offered little steps to help get me there based upon her experiences.

I began to try some of her suggestions in my classroom. I also started going to reading conferences and listening to real people tell about their experiences with literature. It was great.

I knew that it was important to start small, so I began to implement journal writing in my classroom. Wow! I could really see the changes in the children's grammar and sound spelling. I also found that by reading and then writing back to them in their journals, I could actually teach them through the writing. Then I began the response journal that was designed to be used with literature. At the time, I was still using the basal reader; but instead of using so much of the workbook, I had my students respond to what they had read through their journaling. Sometimes it was a free write and other times I posed specific questions to think about and respond to.

Figures 4.4 and 4.5 show two examples of journaling in response to a literature selection read in Barb's second grade class.

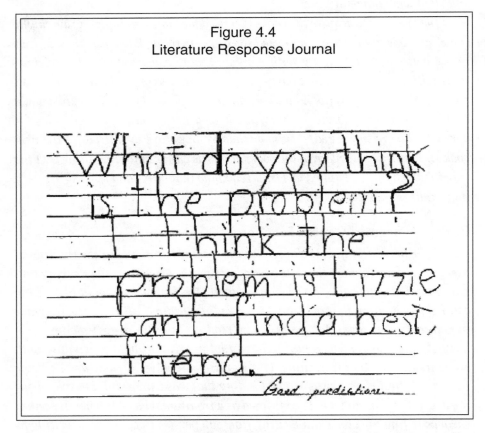

Figure 4.4
Literature Response Journal

> What do you think is the problem? I think the problem is Lizzie cant find a best friend.
>
> *Good prediction.*

My next step was to visit other teachers who were using these strategies to see how they handled reading and writing in their classrooms. I remember being impressed by how few commercially produced materials I saw and that much of what was being used was teacher and child generated. Writing was everywhere, and I noticed how rich the writing was. I saw literature circles in action and knew this was one of things I wanted to try, but still couldn't figure out how.

I knew it was important to model what I wanted them to do, so I created a guide sheet. I then made small groups and worked with each one as a model. It worked!

For me the blending of literature with the districts existing program has been a slow process. I have read, listened, thought, tried things, thought some more, and remembered to take very small steps. I have worked on this for about five years. My goal has always been to incorporate more trade books, more writing, more child-centered, response-centered activities, and eliminate ability grouping. I feel good about where those five years have taken me. I now have heterogeneous groups. Sometimes certain children will be reading the same book and sometimes we are all reading different books. I have learned how to do similar activities with them in spite of the diversity in materials. One example is doing a story map as they discuss the characters, the setting, the problem in the story, the solutions, and so on.

Incorporating the reading, writing, and trade books together has been a very exciting change for me. I've learned that it can be done, and I know that my teaching and my students learning are so much better as a result of the changes I have made.

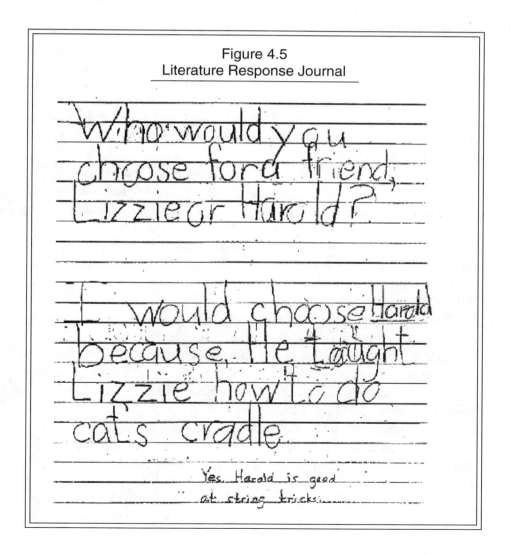

Figure 4.5
Literature Response Journal

Loletta—Third Grade Teacher

My use of literature began twelve years ago with a group of accelerated fifth grade students, but I have since used literature in both third and fourth grades with children of varying reading abilities. I came from a multi-text basal approach in fifth grade to using the core list put forward by the district. My greatest challenge came when I worked with a group of sixteen fourth grade students with reading abilities one to two years below grade level. They were nine years old reading at about the second grade reading level, and I had no materials!

The district was in a transition period where three commercial programs were being piloted. I had no desire to use those programs, and since my district had not said, "Thou shalt not use trade books, I decided that was the way in which I would work with these students.

I had to ask myself, "What is the very best thing I can do for this group of kids?" I knew it was unrealistic to believe that I was going to help them make great strides in nine months that they hadn't made in the last four years. These kids had been through some rough times, and I thought that the best thing I could do for them was to teach them to love books. If I could accomplish that in nine months, I had done a lot! The administration was not at all hesitant because they knew it was a difficult group, and they had confidence that I could do a good job with them.

The first week I met them in small groups over lunch. I did interviews and reading and writing surveys where I acted as the scribe. We talked about what they liked to read and what they wanted to do this year. I explained in a way they could understand that we had standards from the state, the guidelines from the school district, as well as expectations from within our building. They understood what we needed to concentrate on this year in terms of what they needed to be able to do at the end of fourth grade. "So how do you want to do it?" I asked. "How should we approach the task?"

I immediately discovered that these students were not at all used to being asked what they wanted to do. Other primary teachers had used literature with students, but because these kids were Title I and more than one third had been identified as learning disabled, they had been getting special attention centering around skills work. They had great trouble articulating who they were as readers and writers. They just didn't know.

I can remember in one early interview, I asked about their first memories of reading. "How did you learn to read?" Although there were a few who could remember some of their early experiences with reading, for the most part they didn't have the same kind of memories about early reading that other students who are readers and writers have. I asked them to talk about what they thought their problems were in reading. We talked a lot about how they thought we might be able to change that.

The other thing I believed about this group was that even though they could not read on the fourth grade level, they were still fourth graders and would have the same interests as other fourth graders. I tried to think about how I could build a reading program around these truths.

I began with a book called A Taste of Blackberries *(Smith, 1973) which I had multiple copies of. I quickly discovered it was way too hard for them to read, so we did some very brief read alouds. I had them do some very brief reader's log sort of responses, and then we made blackberry jam. These were kids who had really disliked reading, and I saw that on this first attempt I had hooked them. They were ready. Through the course of the year, there were times when I chose the books for whole group read aloud. I used Jane Yolen's (1996)* Passager: The Young Merlin Trilogy *and* The Music of Dolphins *(Hesse, 1996), in spite of the fact that these were books they could never pick up and read themselves. I did a read aloud every day to be sure they were getting good literature and a good model for reading. We also did deeper thinking activities including character analysis. I was surprised by the depth of thinking of many of the students. I thought about that a lot. Because they can't read most of them learn auditorily, so perhaps they listen to and watch television more critically than some other kids who are readers. As a result, as I was reading aloud, they were there with the goods.*

In addition, we did echo reading, partner reading, choral reading, songs, and poetry. We did a lot of vocabulary building this way. I never really pushed independent, silent reading because the children in this group were so needy they needed to hear another voice. I had to design my literature program to meet the needs of my students. There were some folks who believed I needed to do more phonics work with these kids, so I approached that through rhymes and poetry and they responded fairly well to that.

Keep in mind that because so many of the students in the group had been identified as Title I, I also had the Title I teacher come into my classroom and support my teaching. The learning support teacher did the same thing. We did reading and writing in many forms with a number of different adults assisting us from time to time. We even included some parents assisting after I sent a note home asking if they could come in and read to or listen to the children read to them. During the course of the year, I had five or six parents who had helped intermittently.

What was not negotiable in this program was that these children, in spite of their reading difficulties, be exposed to a wide range of genres and that that they individually read to me every two or three days. The children knew that there were certain things we needed to accomplish and do in certain ways. I had designed the reading program that way, but choice also entered into what we did. As we looked at what we needed to accomplish, I would often ask them how they wanted to approach it. I remember two studies they chose—one was natural disasters and the other with fantasy.

We gathered information from the library, some were too difficult for them to read independently and other materials that were not. We read and read and read and then, following a written rubric, they were expected to do a written report and an oral report. We did a lot of videotaping and critiquing of their work. Before long we had double columns for the rubric chart where both the teacher rated the students and then the students also rated themselves.

From this experience, I learned that even with less than stellar readers, using literature works. They did become better readers and actively engaged in writing that they were eager to share. They did move to be more independent learners and decision makers. Each of these children had been bitten by the bug to want to read more. I had not made them the readers we all wished they could be, but I had achieved my goal of making reading a more positive experience for them.

John—A Fourth Grade Teacher

I use the reading workshop with my students, but it is important to know this is only one of the ways I organize my reading program. I am required to use the commercial program adopted by the district, and the fourth grade has also adopted certain core books. In addition, I have certain thematic units I use that are based on the integration of literature into other units we are expected to teach in fourth grade. So, as you can see, my reading program is a combination of many things. Now for me that's great because I can pick and choose how I will teach reading this week or this month. It does take some extra planning, but I have had such a positive response from my students, from the most gifted reader to the less able reader, that I can't imagine going back to the regular, straight basal reader day in and day out. I guess, put simply, it just didn't meet the needs of my students or me.

Because I use so many approaches to teach reading, I would recommend that teachers start small and simple. Stay with what you are doing for most of your program and try leaving that for a few weeks and implementing something else such as a literature unit or reading workshop. In that way, you are not totally overwhelmed and you are still keeping the administration and curriculum coordinator happy that you have not completely left the district's plan for teaching reading.

I have found that school districts want children to learn how to read but aren't too. concerned with how you reach that goal. Wandering off the basal path for a week or two here and there hasn't been seen as a problem.

I want them to love reading and want to do it even when it isn't reading class in school. When I began, I spent two days a week with reading workshops. I did that for the whole school year and my children came to understand that Tuesday and Thursday were reading workshop days. It was just amazing how much they looked forward to those days. I have been a teacher for about 15 years now and it has been an evolution. I'm happy where I am now, but I know I won't stay here. I'll keep what works and try new things all the time. One thing I can say without question is that using literature with my students has not only helped them really look forward to reading and be good readers, it has helped me to love teaching just as much (and maybe even more) today than I did 15 years ago!

Can This Work with the Existing School Program?

This is perhaps one of the questions teachers ask most frequently. Probably because of two things. Many districts still adhere to some form of commercial reading program that is the core of the curriculum. Consequently, teachers need to work around existing expectations of the school board, administration, and curriculum coordinators. This is certainly an important consideration.

Another reason for the question probably stems from teachers' uncertainty—Can I do this? Will I like it once I try it? Is it something I will want to continue over time? Many feel uncomfortable letting go of the tried and familiar before they are sure about using literature. This is more than understandable; it is smart!

The beauty of using literature in your classroom is that it can be woven into the existing program in any number of ways. Maybe you are a teacher who wants to start using some of the organizational strategies presented in this book with the literature in your reading anthology series adopted by the district. Fine! Many of the ideas presented in this book will allow you to do that with minimal change. On the other hand, you might be the teacher who wants to move to a more literature-focused approach. The tools for that are here, too.

One important message that I cannot stress enough has also been touched upon by each of the 26 teachers I have talked to in preparation for writing this book—start slowly and take small steps. Even though you might personally love a good story, believe in what quality literature can offer your students, and fantasize about many things you might try in your classroom, you probably have never actually put all of this into practice. Jumping into this approach without designing a plan, considering what the obstacles are, and deciding how to blend the existing program with the changes you want to make, can only lead to disaster.

Consider the analogy of the swimming pool. Like one who is just learning to swim, you must begin in the shallow end of the pool. Later, after much experimentation and practice, you will be ready to go off the diving board. The same is true about implementing literature into your reading program. You must begin in the shallow end and hold onto the edge of the pool until you are ready. Once you are comfortable in the water and have tried a little venturing out on your own, you will feel more confident in the deeper end. Over time, trial and error, talking with other teachers, reading and attending professional development workshops and conferences, and being a careful observer of your students' responses, you will be ready to go off the board! Although there may be a tingle in your toes and a few butterflies in your stomach, you know you can do it and the attempt is made. Just as your first dive will probably not be "6.0," you land it and you continue to refine your technique and practice your skills. Using literature is much the same. We never stop learning, because every year our students are different, there are more wonderful books from which to choose, and we are a little more knowledgeable ourselves because of past experiences. We continue to grow as do our students. Learning never stops.

So, make some plans today. Consider all the variables that direct the changes you make and start small as you move slowly ahead. Both you and your students will be glad you did.

Some Final Thoughts

Moving away from what you have done for years and toward the use of literature in your reading program is not always an easy journey. There is no recipe, formula, or blueprint to follow. I cannot recommend one teacher to observe, any particular book to read, or class to take that will make it simple. It is about listening to yourself and sometimes thinking out loud. It is sharing with and bouncing ideas off of colleagues. It's about being a reflective practitioner—look back on what you've done and ask yourself, "How did it go and how can I make it better?" It's about being what Ken Goodman (1996) has coined a "kid watcher." How have they responded to the ways in which you teach reading? Are you satisfied with what you see? What kind of response do you get from your best and often loudest critics (your students) as you implement new ways to use literature?

You will find that you may ask a lot of questions and may not always get the quick answers you wish for. You may need to carefully examine your thoughts and beliefs about children and reading. Is a philosophical shift in order? Such decisions are sometimes painful because of the changes we experience. It should be very thoughtful and personal. It is more than implementing ideas, you must believe in them first.

As you begin to consider changes, even small ones, I encourage you to collaborate and share your thoughts, successes, failures, and ideas with colleagues. Talk to other teachers, go to conferences, read professionally, observe students, take risks, continue to evolve, and stay energized. Know that there is no perfect lesson, classroom, or teacher. We learn from our mistakes, life goes on, and hopefully we improve as a result of our experiences.

Finally, I ask that you move slowly and thoughtfully as you transport yourself and your students toward a more effective and active use of literature in the classroom. And as you travel toward your goal, enjoy the ride (and the books, too)!

References

Chall, J. (1967). *Learning to read: The great debate*. New York: McGraw Hill.

Chall, J. (1989). Learning to read: The great debate 20 years later. *Phi Delta Kappan, 70*, 521–538.

Flesch, R. (1956). *Why Johnny can't read*. New York: Harper and Brothers.

Goodman, K. (1986). *What's whole in whole language*. Portsmouth, NH: Heinemann.

Goodman, K. (1996). *On reading*. Portsmouth, NH: Heinemann.

O'Malley, J. (1997). Considering the sources and the resources. *Book Links, 6*, 5.

Routman, R. (1988). *Transitions: From literature to literacy*. Portsmouth, NH: Heinemann.

Routman, R. (2000). *Conversations: Strategies for teaching, learning, and evaluating*. Portsmouth, NH: Heinemann.

Smith, F. (1979). *Reading without nonsense*. New York: Teacher's College Press.

Stanovich, K. (1986). Matthew effects in reading: Some consequences of individual differences in early reading acquisition. *Reading Research Quarterly, 21*, 360–407.

Zarillo, J. (1989). Teachers' interpretation of literature-based reading. *The Reading Teacher, 43*, 22–28.

Children's Books

Brink, C. R. (1970). *Caddie Woodlawn*. New York: Macmillan. [Originally published in 1935].

Carroll, L. (1963). *Alice's adventures in Wonderland*. New York: Macmillan [Originally published in 1866].

Fisher, A. (1971). *Feathered ones and furry*. New York: Crowell.

Hesse, K. (1996). *The music of dolphins*. New York: Scholastic.

Lowrey, L. (1995). *Anastasia, absolutely*. New York: Houghton Mifflin.

Maclachlan, P. (1985). *Sarah, plain and tall*. New York: Harper Row.

Smith, D. B. (1973) *A taste of blackberries*. New York: Crowell.

Taylor, M. (1976). *Roll of thunder, hear my cry*. New York: Dell.

Wilder, L. I. (1953). *Little house in the big woods*. New York: Harper & Row. [Originally published in 1866].

Yolen, J. (1996). *Passager: The young Merlin trilogy*. New York: Harcourt Brace.

5

Choosing Appropriate
Books and Activities

She got off the suitcase and opened it up right there on the sidewalk.

Jeffrey gasped. "Books!"

Books all right. Both sides of the suitcase crammed with them. Dozens more than anyone would ever need for homework.

Jeffrey fell to his knees. He and Amanda and the suitcase were like a rock in a stream; the school-goers just flowed to the left and the right around them. He turned his head this way and that to read the titles...."My library," Amanda Beale said proudly.

Jerry Spinelli, 1990, p. 11

You probably won't be carrying your personal collection of books in a suitcase as Amanda Beale did, but wouldn't it be wonderful to get such a spirited and enthusiastic response from your students when you share your books with them? Through careful selection of quality books with real kid appeal, you can expect your students to respond with eagerness and fervor.

When I meet teachers in my graduate courses, at conferences, or in the schools I visit, many of them are a lot like Amanda Beale. They want to have a collection of wonderful books, but they also describe how difficult it is to learn about the many new books coming out each year. They aren't quite sure what to put in "their suitcase." This chapter is designed to give you "tools" for good book selection.

Selecting Quality Books

You will have the challenging job of selecting quality books that will be of interest to your students. Teachers need to remember that not all books are good choices. Some are excellent, some are mediocre, and as some would say, there are those not worth the paper on which they are printed. So with thousands of new books coming out every year, and many existing books in your school and classroom libraries, just how does a teacher begin the selection process?

Teachers who are recent graduates of a teacher preparation program have no doubt had a children's literature course in recent years. They are fortunate to be familiar with so much of the newest and hopefully the best in the world of children's literature and will recognize contemporary book authors and illustrators. But, as with any body of information, it is quickly outdated as new books are written and fresh, new authors emerge. Therefore, what is most important to all teachers, both the novice and the seasoned veteran, is that they all have the necessary skills to select appropriate books today and in the future.

We owe it to our students to offer them books we know to be the best! But what do we look for as we attempt to find those outstanding selections?

First and foremost, we must remember that not everyone likes everything. So even when we use some standards by which to select books, we will find that not every student is impressed with our selections. You know the old adage, "You can't please all the people all the time." It's certainly true with book selection.

However, there are some guidelines to follow. First, all children (and adults, too!) look for a good strong story. The plot should be well-paced, have a problem that needs to be solved, be action-oriented, and have a satisfactory conclusion that does not leave the reader hanging. Several favorites that offer this to the reader include *Mirette on the High Wire (McCully, 1992)*, *Office Buckle and Gloria* (Rathman, 1995), and *The Many Troubles of Andy Russell* (Adler, 1998). Children will want to read a quality book again and again.

Children in all grades can appreciate the beautiful art and distinctive illustrations found in good picture books. Whether the cut paper work of David Wisniewski's Caldecott Medal winner, *Golem* (1996); the oil paints and scratchboard illustrations in the *Faithful Friend* (Pinkney, 1995); the realism of Paul O. Zelinsky's *Rapunzel* (1997); or the various forms of colorful paper craft seen in Denise Fleming's *In the Small, Small Pond* (1993), the illustrations always garner the attention of children looking for a good book to read.

Teachers should not underestimate the power of humor and unusual story lines. What could be more enjoyed than the ridiculous situations found in books like Martin Waddell's (1996) *What Use is A Moose?*, David Small's (1985) *Imogene's Antlers*, or Dav Pilkey's (1994) very funny *Dog Breath*? Children have a remarkable and delightful sense of humor, and they find many of today's selections to be absolutely knee slapping stories. Consider the sense of humor of the age with which you are working and select books that "tickle their funnybone."

Variety and Balance

When assembling the literature center in your classroom, be certain to include a variety of books. From the make believe of fantasy to the "this is like my life" of realistic fiction, from the rhythm and sometimes rhyme of poetry to the accuracy of historical fiction, from the rich literary tradition of the oldest folktales passed down over generations to the fascinating facts and bits of information offered in the exciting non-fiction written today, variety is indeed one of the beauties of literature.

Don't forget those books which don't seem to fit into a particular genre, like the joke books that adults quickly tire of but children read over and over again the predictable books that the youngest readers just love, or the alphabet and counting books that today have taken on unique characteristics that make them great fun for student and adult audiences. Alphabet and counting books should be included for younger readers to reinforce the concepts they teach, but should also be considered for older audiences. Today, there are many alphabet and counting books that offer interesting challenges for those who already have an understanding of the alphabetic and numeric principles. Look for these for your second, third, and fourth grade classrooms.

Children of all ages like poetry. It often has a musical quality that attracts children and adults alike and appeals to our emotions. The words can suggest new and different images and open the reader to fresh insights. It is the language of emotions and can often draw a deep response from only a few words. Don't be a teacher who is afraid or unsure of poetry. Read it often to your students. A poem is usually quick, gets the attention of the students, and can serve to be the "quieting down" mechanism needed after 30 minutes in a noisy cafeteria or an invigorating recess. Why not open your day or perhaps your science unit on weather with a poem? Let your students see you enjoying poetry not just as an isolated unit, but integrated into your teaching. Chapter 6 will introduce several examples of poetry activities to try in your classroom.

Reading Levels

We must be certain the books we select represent a wide variety of reading levels. As teachers, we know if children perceive a book as too difficult, they won't give it a try; while on the other hand, a book that appears too easy won't get into the hands of children either. And remember, a child's listening reading level is always higher than his independent reading level. Therefore, teachers might choose to have certain books in the classroom collection that they know would not be good choices for self-selected independent reading, but excellent choices for a read aloud. Anticipate a wide range of reading levels in your classroom rather than adhering to the old-fashioned "grade-level reader" idea. Students selecting a book which they can comfortably read and enjoy is what really matters, not the grade level someone has prescribed for the book.

Many teachers have overcome the obstacle that readability presents by implementing a more balanced reading program. This may include the teacher reading aloud, shared reading (where students read along with the teacher who serves as a reading model), paired reading (where partners take turns reading and following), listening to readings on a tape recorder (as the student follows along in the book,) whole class or small group guided reading (the teacher meeting with a group of children to talk, think, and question their way through a book or part of a book), individualized guided reading (students self-select the text and self-pace their reading followed by individual conferences with the teacher), and independent reading (in which the teacher's role changes from initiating and modeling to observing and responding). By varying "the way" your students read, you can reduce readability problems.

Before telling children that a book is too hard for them, remember that they will often want to go a little beyond their independent level (meaning they can recognize 95 percent of the words). Maybe they are interested because they heard the story and want to read it again, because a friend read it, or merely because they want the challenge of reading a harder book. As the teacher, you might instead suggest a grouping strategy that would support the reading of that particular selection. For instance, by encouraging paired reading or shared reading, you can satisfy the interest of the child as well as reaffirm the child's desire to read in spite of reading difficulties. Motivation is very powerful, and sometimes if the motivation and engagement in the book is high, the child can rise to the challenge. Children often surprise us.

Read Alouds

A teacher reading aloud to the class is something we naturally see when visiting a kindergarten or first grade classroom, but as we move through the grades, we see less and less of this. There are many positive outcomes of reading aloud including sparking interest in books and reading, modeling appropriate reading behaviors including reading with expression and fluency, and sharing literature that the child might not otherwise choose to read independently. Also, a natural outgrowth of reading aloud is the nurturing of language development and comprehension skills, and a better understanding of the functions and conventions of print.

In its report "Becoming a Nation of Readers," the Commission on Reading declared, "There is no substitute for a teacher who reads children good stories" (Anderson, Hiebert, Scott, Wilkinson, 1985). This book and author support reading aloud as an essential part of every day in every grade. "But, what's the point," Mrs. Webb, a fourth grade teacher, asked when I questioned her about reading aloud to her 10 and 11 year olds. "They can all read well enough to read themselves."

Yes, when you are a 10 or 11 year old, you probably have developed adequate skills to read yourself, but that doesn't mean a child of this age wouldn't simply delight being read to by his or her teacher. Whether a successful or struggling reader, a young child or an adult, we all enjoy and look forward to the sometimes soothing, sometimes exciting, but always enjoyable chance to hear a story read aloud.

Michael Tunnell and James Jacobs (1989) report in a research review of literature-based reading programs that "daily reading aloud from enjoyable trade books has been the key that unlocked literacy growth" for many students (p. 475). Another study by Feitelson, Kita, and Goldstein (1986) found that first graders who were read to for 20 minutes each day outscored comparable groups in decoding, reading comprehension, and active use of language. Therefore, reading aloud is more than just entertaining and more than merely providing students with an excellent model for reading, reading aloud makes better readers. So grab a book and read to your class every day!

For teachers, time is always an issue and especially in the upper elementary grades where teachers talk of the additional content which must be taught in a given school year. One simple solution to this dilemma is to use books that tie into your themes and topics in social studies and science. In this way, you offer your students all the benefits of the read aloud experience as well as providing opportunities for them to learn about concepts, time periods, events, and people they may be studying. Whether a beautiful poem or a good story is read aloud for sheer enjoyment or is carefully woven into the context of a science or social studies lesson, book read-alouds can play a very essential part in school curricula.

Offering Diversity

Books can offer readers so much, but in particular they offer children an opportunity to see the world in a more global or broader sense. Many would call the books described in this section "multicultural books." I prefer to call them books that support and reflect diversity. I do so because too often, when teachers think of the word "multicultural," they define it in a more narrow sense to include books that show people of color and minority cultures. Others have defined multicultural literature as being about people who are not in the mainstream populations (Cai and Bishop, 1994). I tend to look at this literature more broadly, since I see it supporting diversity of all kinds. This includes race and culture as well as the diverse perspectives of gender and gender roles, age, ability, exceptionalities, alternate family structures, and social diversity.

About ten years ago, as I spoke to a group about the importance of using such diverse literature the classroom, I overheard Peg, a kindergarten teacher, talking to a fellow teacher. This is what Peg told her colleague.

> I live in an almost all white, rural community. Many of my students will get jobs in the area and stay close to home. There really is no need for me to use this kind of literature. We do not live in a multicultural area. It's more important to use it in the city schools where kids see other races and need to understand each other.

How would you respond to what this teacher believed? Which children would benefit most from exposure to literature that supports diversity?

I got to know Peg that day, and I felt she was a good teacher in many ways. I also believe that Peg misunderstood the value of books I spoke about. She failed to see all that they have to offer every child from every community, large or small, rural or urban. Literature plays a vital role in providing vicarious experiences in interacting with others—whether those we interact with are like ourselves or quite different. Whether children live in a mono-racial community or not, differences of all sorts surround them every day. Books can help share, understand, and appreciate those differences. As teachers, we need to remember that we are preparing children to live in a diverse and pluralistic world where they can appreciate both the similarities and differences we find in each other. Quality books can enlarge their small world and help make this possible.

Needs and Interests of the Audience

Perhaps, two of the most important questions we need to ask ourselves when selecting books is "Who will read it?" and "Why?" The interests of your audience are extremely important in the selection process. Just as you have preferences when you select the books you read, so do your students. Watch to see the kinds of books they read and the authors and illustrators that pique their interests. Not all children in any grade level are alike, but many of the kindergarten and primary children you may work with will enjoy make-believe (fantasy) stories, animal stories, and stories about children who have the same experiences they have. Older children in third and fourth grade continue to enjoy animal stories, but also enjoy nature, adventure, science, and mystery selections.

Many students will be interested in a book or topic that you recommend. When you find a book you believe would be a "real hit" with your class, do a book talk or a book jackdaw. A book talk is similar to a preview you might see at the movie theater before the main attraction begins. It shows you short snippets to interest you, make you more curious, whet your appetite, and entice you into coming back to see more. A good book talk does exactly that, too. As you present a book talk, give only limited information rather than all the details of the book. Many of us who are fans of the television series Reading Rainbow, are familiar with the segment where children give booktalks. If the kids can do it— then so can we!

A book jackdaw, another variation of a book talk, is named after the bird known as the jackdaw (also commonly called the grackle). This bird is easily attracted to objects it finds and carries them back to its nest. To do a jackdaw, you should have a script (what you want to say about the book) as well as a few simple props to get the interest of the audience. Like the bird, you need to "carry back to your nest" (classroom) a few especially interesting items that relate to your book. They don't have to be at all elaborate. In fact, simple is better. Together, your props and your script will spark interest in even the most difficult to motivate child. A sample of the script and props used in a jackdaw done in a second grade classroom, appear in Figure 5.1.

Figure 5.1
Book Jackdaw

Moosetache by Margie Palatine

Required props:
- a very long paper mustache (each piece at least one foot long)
- tape
- scissors
- comb or brush

Before beginning the script, tape the long paper mustache on your upper lip.

Script:
"Oh, my goodness. What a mess I have here. This is indeed a real problem (continually wrestle with the mustache that is always getting in your way). I guess by now you have recognized what my problem is, but we have not been formally introduced. My

cont.

name is Moose and as you can see, my problem is my incredibly long moosetache! (Hold up comb, brush, scissors one at a time.) I have tried everything. I have combed it and brushed it, I've plucked it and snipped it, but this mustache just can't be controlled and it is really getting in my way.

With a long mustache like this it's hard to dance and I love dancing! It's almost impossible to cook and keep my moosetache out of the food, and I just adore cooking! And it is especially hard to ski because I can't see where I am going, and I just love to ski! So what's a moose with a moosetache to do? Do you have any ideas? Well, to see if any of your ideas might work and to find out if I ever solve this "mooseincredible" problem, you'll just have to read this very funny book by Margie Palatini called *Moosetache*. I guarantee it'll really have you laughing about these amazing "mooseunderstood" whiskers.

Research has shown that children are more likely to develop as readers when they are reading content that interests them (Early, 1993). Get to know the children in your class. What do they talk about? What do they seen interested in? Become a good "kid watcher," and you will be surprised by what you learn from your students about your students.

The Literary Elements

What makes a good book? Another of the primary considerations when evaluating a piece of literature are the literary elements including plot, characterization, setting, theme, style, and point of view. Although there is much that could be said about each of these "parts of a body of a book," quite simply, we must be sure the book offers the reader an engaging story that describes clearly what the characters do and what happens to them. This is the fabric of the story and without an engaging and intriguing plot—there is no story to read. For young children, plots should be linear and sequential. Older students can understand a story that has several plot lines and may skip from the here and now to the past or the future. Be careful that you consider the age and developmental level of the students in your classroom before you offer them a story that might be confusing.

In addition to a great story, we need memorable characters who are convincingly real and lifelike. These are the "friends" children will come to know. Some we will love and some we will despise. With young children, characters are typically flat and one dimensional. In the 32–48 pages of most picture books, they have little room to grow and develop. Those who are good characters remain good and those who are bad seldom change during the course of the story. However, as children move into even the easy chapter books, we find that characters can and do change as the story develops. We learn about them, one piece at a time, just as we do the real people we encounter every day. We learn about them through their actions, their dialogues, and monologues, as well as through their interactions with others in the story. Alex, a seven year old who enjoyed the *Song and Dance Man* (Ackerman, 1988), described the children in the book in this way; "I would really like to be one of those kids because they have a grandpa they can go visit. I think he lives real close. My gramps lives far away so I don't get to go to his house so much." It is obvious that this child made a real connection with these characters as he read. Other books with strong and memorable characters include Hoffman's (1991) *Amazing Grace* and the delightful bear and hare in Jan Steven's *Tops and Bottoms* (1995).

The setting of the story helps the reader/listener know what the characters know and see what the characters see. Whether it be the prairie during early days of stagecoach travel, a small rural town during segregation in the south, a secret garden, a plane crash at the edge of the wilderness, a big city being torn apart by riot and fire, or an old house with squeaks and sounds that could only be made by lingering (but friendly) ghosts, the setting affects the action and the characters of the story. Whether real as in Donald Hall's *Ox-Cart Man* (1979) or the imaginary world of Narnia in C. S. Lewis's (1961) *The Lion, the Witch and the Wardrobe*, the setting must be carefully crafted to create a believable story for the reader. Other books that seem to "take you there" because of the rich and clearly described setting include Rylant's (1982) *When I Was Young in the Mountains* and *Wagon Wheels* (Brenner, 1978).

Earlier we asked ourselves, "Why is the child reading this story?" Taking that into consideration will help us match child and book more easily. Another question to ponder when selecting books is "Why did the author write the story?" Is there some message or underlying theme the writer hopes to convey?" Perhaps, on the surface, a book seems to be an amusing fantasy about barnyard animals who live together and a spider who saves a pig—imagine that! But is there more? Does it help the reader see the power and importance of true friendship? The meaning of loneliness? The acceptance of death?

When selecting books, think about appropriate themes for the age of your students. Think about the use of symbolism in some books and whether your students can understand it. Whether implicit or explicit, a message that is concrete or more abstract, themes such as cooperation, overcoming fear or prejudice, acceptance and understanding of self, friendship, or supporting and helping one another are just some of the themes which can spread across many age levels and be significant and meaningful to children.

We also need to look closely at the way in which the author uses words in presenting the story. Does the writer use words that paint startling and clear images as does Paul Goebel (1978) in *The Girl Who Loved Wild Horses* when he describes the stallion's eyes as "cold stars" and his tail and mane as "whispy clouds?" Are the words so descriptive that readers "see" the actions in their mind's eye as nine-year-old Missie did as she read *Owl Moon* (Yolan, 1987). She told her teacher, "When I read words like 'footprints in the snow follow us' and 'shadows bumped after me' it seemed like I could really see it happening."

Maybe the author has chosen to use the singsong cadence of repetitive phrases such as "When I was young in the mountains" or the words from *There Was an Old Lady Who Swallowed a Fly* (Tabak, 1997) that you can't seem to get out of your head! Whether a repetitive phrase, the use of figurative language, insightful and vivid depictions, or words that are more lyrical in nature, consider the author's style as you pick and choose books that will become favorites your students.

The final literary element we will discuss is the point of view or the perspective from which the story is told. Is it a storyteller as in *Stone Soup* (Brown, 1947) who appears to be all knowing (omniscient) and therefore tells the tale from "inside" the heads of characters? In this way, the writer more closely identifies with a particular character and tells the story as though he sees it through the eyes of that character. Phyllis Naylor does this in *Shiloh* (1991) as she speaks through not only the lips, but the eyes and the heart of Marty. The most direct way to tell a story is through the first person narrative point of view. This is easily identifiable through the use of "I" as in the book *Missing May* (Rylant, 1992) and *Catherine Called Birdy* (Cushman, 1994).

Availability of Books

Now that you have some "tools" to help you make good choices in books, there is more to consider. Do you have a wide variety of books available to your students? If not, the bigger question is "Where and how will you get them?"

Many teachers have few books available because the expense of building a classroom library falls solely on the teacher. Other classrooms have a multitude of books, but of such poor quality that they offer no "invitation" to read. I observed this situation during a recent visit to a first grade classroom. As the children finished their previous lesson, I heard the teacher encourage them to "find a book and read it." I noticed that the children seemed to have no interest in the shelf of books to which she referred. Some of the students sharpened pencils, got a drink, looked in their desk, checked on the gerbil in his cage, and investigated a number of other activities in the classroom. No one came to the bookshelf at all! I took a handful of books for a closer look. Although I perused them quickly and unsystematically, I could see why these books had no appeal for the students. Of the fourteen I examined, ten were written before 1975 and had illustrations that appeared dated and seven were such difficult reading that these six and seven-year-olds would have been unable to read them. In addition, many were badly torn and visually unappealing. I was able to find only four that would be the kind of books that would call out to the child and offer an enjoyable reading experience.

One easy and inexpensive way to obtain a good, hands-on classroom library is to make arrangements with your school librarian to have a new collection of books on loan in your classroom every few weeks throughout the year. This can be done by the classroom teacher going to the library to hand select the books or by the librarian "pulling" certain books that seem appropriate for the class. This book collection can even be customized to reflect interests of your students or the content in upcoming lessons. In this way, there is no added expense to maintaining a classroom library with a continuous source of new and interesting books.

The children's book clubs (such as Scholastic, Trumpet, Carnival, and Troll) also make building a library through bonus points within the realm of possibility for classroom teachers. As your children purchase books, you collect bonus points. It is an easy way to create or replenish a classroom library or even begin to collect "sets" of books to use when you begin to integrate literature in to your reading program.

Accessibility

You might be very adept at selecting good books and have a wide variety of choices in your classroom, but if quality books are not accessible to your students they serve very little purpose. What exactly do we mean by "accessible"? Let's look at Mrs. Intiman's class for an example.

Mrs. Intiman had a wall of low bookshelves under the windows that ran the length of her classroom. One set of shelves held art supplies, another student games and toys, and the shelves behind her desk held many books. She often selected a book form this shelf to read aloud. When she finished the reading, she returned the book to the same shelf. There was another smaller bookshelf filled with books that were visibly tattered and unkept. Students were permitted to read books from what she called "their bookshelf," but the students could not take books from what was called "the teacher's bookshelf." When Mrs. Intiman was asked about this arrangement she was quick to answer—"If the kids would use the books from my book shelf, then in no time at all, they would look like the ones on their shelf." In Mrs. Intiman's efforts to preserve the books, she sent a strong and inappropriate message. What do you think it was?

If we believe accessibility to merely mean that books are present in the classroom, then we could say that most classrooms would meet this definition. However, if we define accessibility as meaning that good books are present and easily available for students' use in the classroom, then, it seems, the accessibility of books is less often the case. A number of research studies validate accessibility as a factor that affects early interest in and success in reading (Morrow, 1991). In spite of these findings, we seem to give more importance to book availability, but less thought to book accessibility in the classroom

Format

The format of the book includes the way in which it is put together. From the binding of the book, it's size, length of chapters, and the size of print, the way the book looks will directly influence whether it can be easily used in you classroom. The print should be appropriate for your students to read easily. The best arrangement of pictures and words will differ depending upon the age and needs of your students. Do you want to invest in a hard cover binding which may last for years and stand up to heavy use, or would you prefer instead to have a smaller initial investment that allows you to change the titles you use more frequently? All of these questions are important to consider in the process of book selection.

Additional Considerations

Although these may at first seem like unimportant details, they are all things teachers should consider when selecting books for students. The criteria by which we evaluate a children's book depends to a great extent upon the type of book we are considering. This chapter has offered some general guidelines, but specific criteria are needed for certain types of books. For instance, in picture books, there should be a marriage between the pictures and the words—do they work well together and support each other? A fantasy has to allow the reader to "buy into" the story and go along for the ride. If it is well written it can transport us to that imaginary land or to meet those preposterous characters. Historical fiction requires authenticity in every detail especially the setting.

Now that we know how to get quality books into the hands of our students, let's discuss what's next.

What Can I do With the Books I Choose?

Read books to your students every day, whether they are unable to read themselves or are avid and accomplished readers. Find ways to make books accessible to your students and integrate them into your teaching through a story read aloud each day, a time set aside for SSR when everyone reads (even the teacher), or literature used in your reading program.

I ask every teacher to remember the aesthetic stance advocated by Louise Rosenblatt which focuses on what the book has aroused in the reader rather than information in the text (see chapter 3).

There are many ways to encourage and supports children's responses to literature. Doing a worksheet or other pencil/paper activities of sometimes mindless and often repetitive tasks will rarely encourage students to "get into" the book they have read. Workbooks and black line masters cannot create an atmosphere for reading and responding. Teachers need to allow children to make choices about what and how they will read (alone or with a partner), as well as offering them options for responding. To encourage real thinking, we should offer active, student-centered response activities.

We can also help children make connections through their responses. What you offer could have common threads with math, science, social studies, or other content areas. Allow these activities to bridge the gaps between content areas and make learning more integrated in your classroom.

Through the books we select, we can provide opportunities to build on the interests and prior knowledge of our students. Let children initiate ideas of where they "want to go" and "what they want to accomplish" through their response activities. By giving children some guidelines and allowing them to make choices within those guidelines, we can anticipate many diverse forms of response, more student initiated reading, writing, drama, art, and cross-curricular connections made by their initiatives. These individual contributions can be made in whole group settings if teachers give children the license to share their ideas and are accepting of their responses.

Chapter 6 offers extended options using literature selections falling into important themes found in elementary classrooms. This repertoire of ideas will take your students into writing, art and media making, dramatizing, as well as a number of cross-curricular connections.

What is vitally important as we explore literature response, is that we encourage and support children in how they "experience" a book. What they pictured in their minds, imagined as they met characters, saw as they traveled to another place in time, wondered as they followed the events in the story, or saw as similar to or different from their own experiences should be shared through their responses. And, finally, teachers should remind themselves that, regardless of the organizational framework you use or the degree to which you incorporate literature into your classroom, learning experiences should be centered around reading and the active and personal responses of children.

References

Anderson, R. C., Hiebert, E. H., Scott, J. A., Wilkinson, I. A. G. (1985). *Becoming a nation of readers: The report of the Commission on Reading*. Washington, DC: U.S. Office of Education.

Cai, M., and Bishop, R. S. (1994). "Multicultural literature for children: Towards clarification of the concept." In A. H. Dyson & C. Genishi (Eds.), *The need for story—Cultural diversity in the classroom and the community*. (pp. 57–71). Urbana, IL: National Council of Teachers of English.

Early, M. (1993). "What ever happened to...?" *The Reading Teacher, 46,* 302–308.

Feitelson, D., Kita, B., and Goldstein, Z. (1986). "Effects of listening to series stories on first graders' comprehension and use of language." *Research in the Teaching of English, 20,* 339–355.

Morrow, L. W. (1991). "Promoting voluntary reading." In J. Flood, J. M. Jensen, D. Lapp, and J. R. Squire (Eds.), *Handbook of Research on Teaching the English Language Arts* (pp. 681–690). New York: Macmillan.

Tunnell, M. O., and Jacobs, J. S. (1989). "Using real books: Research findings on literature-based reading instruction." *The Reading Teacher, 42,* 470–477.

Children's Books

Ackerman, K. (1988). *Song and dance man*. New York: Knopf.

Adler, D. A. (1998). *The many troubles of Andy Russell*. New York: Harcourt Brace & Company.

Brenner, B. (1978). *Wagon Wheels*. New York: Harper & Row.

Brown, M. (1947). *Stone soup*. New York: Antheneum.

Cushman, K. (1994). *Catherine, called Birdy*. New York: Clarion.

Fleming, D. (1993). *In a small, small pond*. New York: Henry Holt & Company.

Goebel, P. (1978). *The girl who loved wild horses*. New York: Bradbury.

Hall, D. (1979). *Ox-cart man*. New York: Viking.

Hoffman, M. (1991). *Amazing Grace*. New York: Dial.

Lewis, C. L. (1951). *The lion, the witch, and the wardrobe*. New York: Macmillan.

McCully, E.A. (1992), *Mirette on the high wire*. New York: Putnam.

Naylor, P. (1991). *Shiloh*. New York: Antheneum.

Palatini. M. (1997). *Moosetache*. New York: Scholastic.

Pilkey, D. (1994). *Dog breath: The horrible trouble with Hally Tosis*. New York: Blue Sky.

Pinkney, J. (1995). *Faithful friend*. New York: Henry Holt & Company.

Rathman, P. (1995). *Office Buckle and Gloria*. New York: Putnam.

Rylant, C. (1982). *When I was young in the mountains*. New York: Dutton.

Rylant, C. (1992). *Missing May*. New York: Orchard.

Sendak, M. (1963). *Where the wild things are*. New York: Harper & Row.

Small, D. (1985). *Imogene's antlers*. New York: Crown

Spinelli, J. (1990). *Maniac Magee*. New York: Little Brown and Company.

Stevens, J. (1995). *Tops and bottoms*. New York: Harcourt Brace.

Tabak, S. (1997). *There was an old lady who swallowed a fly*. New York: Scholastic.

Waddell, M. (1996). *What use is a moose?* New York: Candlewick.

Wisniewski, D. (1996). *Golem*. New York: Clarion.

Yolan, J. (1987). *Owl moon*. New York: Philomel.

Zelinsky, P. (1998). *Rapunzel*. New York: Dutton.

Part 4

A Resource for Teachers: Practical Ideas

Teachers are very creative individuals, but also very busy people. It is difficult for teachers to keep abreast of all that is new in the world of literature. As teachers we want to be aware of new books and to develop new ideas and activities to support our literature-rich environments. This requires our being knowledgeable of a variety of sources of information

In the trend toward virtual images and on-line access to information, finding valuable information is easier than ever before. However, you may be asking yourself where should I begin? What changes should I expect in the production and marketing of children's books?

Chapter 6 will provide resources to support teachers as they use technology to research literature related topics. The chapter will begin by introducing teachers to resources that provide an infinite amount of current information about books, authors and illustrators, professional publications, literature related conferences and workshops all available through your home or classroom computer. The second part will offer yet another type of resource—many new books and corresponding kid-tested and teacher approved ideas to support a response-centered, literature-rich environment. This will be done through nine broad themes that frequently appear in the curricula of grades K–4 and 34 specific books (as well as additional related books) that correspond to those themes. Each of the "themed books," offers 3–7 activities (over 125 activities in all)! These literature extensions have been successfully used in classrooms across the United States. Take these ideas and use your creative spirit to adapt them to best meet the needs of your students.

Every effort has been made to extend literature across many different content areas. This is illustrated in Figure 6.1—Literature Across the Curriculum.

Before continuing to explore the resources this chapter offers, a few words about literature extensions are needed. Every effort has been made to move away from what is sometimes referred to as "basalizing" a great piece of literature when we create one worksheet type activity after another. Although there is an occasional pattern or template offered in Appendix A, this author does not recommend that the creation of what one teacher called a "literature pack." This was no more that a set of black line masters, strikingly similar to the diet of workbook pages that characterize some commercial reading programs.

As you examine the many activities suggested in this chapter, consider the variables that will affect your reading program. These include your personal philosophy about how children learn; your students' needs, interests, and abilities; your school district's philosophical stance on reading; your classroom resources; and the age appropriateness of the activities offered. Use your own good judgement to select what is best for you and your students. Consider ways you can make minor modifications to suggested ideas to make them work better in your own classroom or grade level. Look closely not only at the books themselves, but the way in which you organize your program and use these materials. Let these ideas be your springboard into a new approach to reading through literature.

6

Kid-Tested and Teacher-Approved Literature Ideas

Grandpa took Mary Ellen inside away from the crowd. "Now, child I am going to show you what my father showed me, and his father before him," he said quietly.

He spooned the honey onto the cover of one of her books. "Taste," he said, almost in a whisper.

Mary Ellen savored the honey on her book.

"There is such sweetness inside of that book, too!" he said thoughtfully. "Such things as adventure, knowledge and wisdom. But these things do not come easily. You have to pursue them. Just like we ran after the bees to find their tree, so you must also chase these things through the pages of a book!"

Patricia Polacco, 1993, p. 25

In Patricia Polacco's beautiful book, *The Bee Tree* (1993), Mary Ellen's grandfather knew the importance of reading and motivating children to read. Just as important as teaching children to read, it is equally important to encourage them to read and to offer them authentic, response-centered activities to enjoy.

Mary Ellen's grandfather was a wonderful teacher who taught her about the power of books and all the adventure, knowledge, and wisdom they have to offer. You can do the same. You may not take your students on a search through the countryside looking for bee trees, but you can begin by creating that literature-rich environment this book advocates. One of the first steps in this journey is becoming knowledgeable yourself—what new books are now available, what information is available about a particular author your students enjoy, what other formats of a particular book might you use in the classroom such as CD ROM or audio and video tapes, and what are some new and exciting ways to extend a particular book into other content areas?

Although teachers are probably the most imaginative and resourceful people I know, even they sometimes feel that the "creative juices" can run dry. Mrs. Bennett, a first grade teacher said it best.

> You know, after reading the book *Corduroy* (Freeman, 1968) with my kindergarten and first grade students for the last seventeen years and doing the same activity of making his overalls with one button on and one button off, it's time for something new. That's not to say I don't like the story or that it isn't a good piece of literature, but there has to be more out there. I just don't have a good way to find out what else is available.

This chapter was written for teachers who share the feelings of Mrs. Bennett. It offers K–4 teachers information on both "in print" and "on line" resources.

Book Selection Aids

Review Journals and Magazines

Review Journals are one of the best sources of information still found in print. They provide information about new titles and offer reviews by experts in the field of children's literature and by teachers who have used the book in their classrooms. They also offer interviews with authors and illustrators and feature articles dealing with a wide variety of topics specific to literature and children. Journals that deal specifically with children's literature include:

Booklinks

Booklist

Bulletin of the Center for Children's Books (BCCB)

Children's Literature Association Quarterly

Children's Literature in Education

The Horn Book Magazine

The Horn Book Guide

Journal of Children's Literature

The New Advocate

School Library Journal

TALL: Teaching and Learning Literature with Children and
    Young Adults

The following journals are not entirely devoted to children's literature, but they do designate at least a part of their publication to the use of books and book reviews.

Language Arts

Primary Voices: K–6

The Reading Teacher

Teaching ideas and activities that connect to children's literature can be found in the following magazines. Many classroom teachers find these helpful as they design literature extensions.

Bookbag

Instructor

Mailbox (Primary)

Mailbox (Intermediate)

Teaching K–8

The Web: Wonderfully Exciting Books

Book Guides

Although good books can rarely be confined to one category or age-group the following book guides will help you to generally classify books by theme, topic or age.

Berman, M. (1996). *What else should I read: Guiding kids to good books.* Englewood, CO: Libraries Unlimited.

Bowker, R. R. *Children's books in print.* New Providence, NJ: Reed Reference Publishing. (Annual)

Bowker, R. R. *Subject guide to children's books in print.* New Providence, NJ: Reed Reference Publishing. (Annual)

Carroll, F. L. (Ed.). (1992). *More exciting, funny, scary, short, different, and sad books kids like about animals, science, sports, families, songs, and other things.* Chicago: IL: American Library Association.

Freeman, J. (1995). *More books kids will sit still for: A read-aloud guide* (2nd ed.). New York: R. R. Bowker.

Gillespie, J. T. (Ed.). (1998). *Best books for children: Preschool through grade 6.* New York: R. R. Bowker

Gunning, T. G. (1999). *Best books for building literacy in the elementary school.* Boston, MA: Allyn & Bacon.

Harmes, J. M. & Lettow, L. (1996). *Picture books to Enhance the Curriculum.* New York: H. W. Wilson.

Hirsch, E. D. & Holdred, J. (Eds.). (1996). *Books to build on: A grade-by-grade resource guide for parents and teachers.* McHenry, IL: Delta.

Johnson, L. W. (1999). *Secrets of the best choice.* Minneapolis, MN: Bethany House.

Kobrin, B. (1995). *Eyeopeners II: Children's books to answer children's questions about the world around then.* New York: Scholastic.

Laughlin, M. K. (1986). *Developing learning skills through children's literature: An idea book for K–5 classrooms and libraries*. Phoenix, AZ: Oryx Press.

Lewis, V. V. & Mayer, W. M. (1998). *Valerie's and Walter's best books for children: A lively, opinionated guide*. New York: Avon Books.

Lima, C. W. & Lima, J. A. (1998) *A to zoo* (5th ed.). New York: R.R. Bowker.

Lipson, E. R. & Luke, S. (Eds.). (1991). *The new york times parent's guide to the best books for children*. New York: Times Books.

Nuba, H. & Sheiman, D. L. (Eds.). (1998). *Children's literature: Developing good readers*. Levittown, PA: Garland Publishing.

Odean, K. (1998). *Great books for boys: More than 600 books for boys 2 to 14*. New York: Ballentine Books.

Odean, K. (1997). *Great books for girls: More than 600 books to inspire today's girls and tomorrow's women*. New York: Ballentine Books.

Thomas, R. L. (1996). *Connecting cultures: A guide to multicultural literature for children*. New York: R. R. Bowker.

Tomlinson, C. M. (Ed.). (1998). *Children's books from other countries*. Langham, MD: Scarecrow Press.

Toussaint, P. (1999). *Great books for African-American children*. New York: Plume.

West, M. I. (1997). *Everyone's guide to children's literature*. Ft. Atkinson, WI: Highsmith Press.

Video and Audio Formats

Is "in print" being replaced with "on line"? Are these technological changes a help or hindrance to education in general and to reading specifically? What are the positive and negative effects of using technology in relation to literature? These are questions we all ask.

Most teachers are in favor of teaching students technological skills. In order to compete in the global marketplace, the understanding and use of technology is a must. Others would respond that when it comes to reading and literature applications, in the eyes of a child, the technology may supercede the love and enjoyment of the story. They would contend that children who use CDs, audio and video tapes, web pages, and other reading and literature software programs are not fully enjoying and appreciating the literature as they do when using a book. Rather, they are enjoying first and foremost the sound, animation, and color such technological formats offer. This issue will be the subject of ongoing debate at reading conferences, teacher workshops, and in faculty rooms. Whatever opinions and beliefs you bring to the discussion, one thing is certain—technology is here to stay.

A number of commercial companies produce literature selections on both video and audiotapes. Although many of us would agree that "the book is always better than the movie," there are several ways in which video and audio versions can be effectively used.

One such way is sharing the video or audio version after a child has read the book or heard the book read by an adult. This is an excellent way to enjoy the story again and again. When a child "sees" the story a second or third time there is much one can continue to enjoy and discuss.

A second way to enjoy the animation, color, and sound brought to the child through video and audio versions is to use it as an alternative to the poor to mediocre quality of today's television programming for children. These formats allow parents and teachers to substitute a quality children's literature selection for a violence packed superhero tale. This format allows the child to view as much or as little as desired at a setting and young audiences enjoy this flexibility in pace.

The following listing provides the names and addresses of a number of major producers of literature selections in video and audio formats. Any of these companies would be pleased to send you or your school a copy of their most recent catalog.

Weston Woods
12 Oakwood Avenue
Norwark, CT 06850-1318
1-800-243-5020

Filmic Archives
The Cinema Center
Botsford, CT 06404-0386
E-mail: custsrv@filmicarchives.com
1-800-366-1920

Pied Piper
9719 DeSoto Avenue
Chatsworth, California 91311-4409
E-mail: orders@aims-multimedia.com
www.aims-multimedia.com
1-800-367-2467

Live Oak Media
P.O. Box 652
Pine Plains, NY 12567
E-mail: liveoak@taconic.met
1-800-788-1121

Library Video Company
P.O. Box 580
Catalog K-32
Wynnewood, PA 19096
E-mail: lbraryvideo.com
1-800-843-3620

SVE & Churchill Media
6677 Northwest Highway
Chicago, IL 60631-1304
www.SVEmedia.com
1-800-829-1900

Teacher's Video Company
P.O. Box ELL-4455
Scottsdale, AZ 85261
1-800-262-8837

Information from the Internet

This age of multimedia has made it possible to have a wealth of information easily within our reach. That, in itself, has made technology a real asset to education and educators. Web sites relating to children's literature are plentiful. The following sites were active at the time of this writing and offered valuable information on books, authors, and related activities to extend the literature experience.

American Library Association–http://www.ala.org/ and www.ala.org/alsc/index.html
The ALA has much information available about its range of services. The second site noted deals specifically with children and contains notable books, awards, and cool sites for kids, and resources for teachers and librarians.

Amazon—http://www.amazon.com/
Whether you are hoping to buy books or simply wanting to learn more about them here's a site full of information. Search for books by author, theme, and age appropriateness. This site does what the card catalogue used to.

Bookwire—http://www.bookwire.com/
Children's best seller lists from Publisher's Weekly, information about conferences and book fairs, authors on tour, and selected features make this a good source of information.

Carol Hurst's Children's Literature Site—http://www.carolhurst.com

One of the best sites you'll find. Designed specifically for those who desire to use books in their classrooms, this site deals with professional topics, author information, book reviews, themes, and a multitude of ideas to connect books with the curriculum. Be sure to subscribe to the free newsletter.

Children's Literature 150 Top Choices—http://www.parentsplace. com/readroom/childnew/top150.html

This site covers a wide variety of topics and includes a focus on books. Feature articles on children's health and nutrition

Children's Literature Authors and Illustrators—http://www.ucet. ufl.edu/~jbrown/chauth.html

This site includes historic and contemporary authors and illustrators. Tips for finding author's addresses are also included.

Children's Literature Web Guide—http://www.acs.ucalgary.ca/ ~dkbrown/index.html

Hundreds of Internet resources related to children's literature are available here. They include book reviews, conferences and book events, publishers and booksellers, authors, reviews, and resources for teachers and parents.

The Discovery Channel—http://discoveryschool.com/schrockguide/

A must see for every elementary teacher! This award-winning site has it all—lesson plans, bulletin board ideas, search engines, and a great literature/language arts section.

Fairrosa Cyber Library—http://www.users.interport.net/~fairrosa/

A great site for information that relates to fanciful books. There are book reviews, articles, discussions, and book lists.

In addition to these specific sites, many children's book publishers have established and maintained their own sites. These are also excellent sources of information about new authors, illustrators and related news and information about children's books. Specific publisher sites include:

www.bdd.com (Bantam Doubleday)
www.harpercollins.com/kids (HarperCollins)
www.simonsays.com/kids/ (Simon & Schuster)
www.penguinputnam.com/index.htm (Penguin Putnam Publishers)
www.scholastic.com/ (Scholastic Books)

Thematic Literature Extensions
Across the Curriculum

The teachers I meet always seem excited to be introduced to new books and ideas for using those books in their classrooms. The following pages include books that have primarily been published in the last several years (with a few exceptions that are so good, I couldn't eliminate them merely because they are more than a few years old). For each book, the reader will find the bibliographic information, age appropriateness, a brief summary, a list of 3–7 activities, and a list of theme related books. Figure 6.1, Literature Across the Curriculum, shows the related content areas of the more than 125 response-centered literature extensions.

But first, a word of caution is needed. The old adage of "more is not better" is important to remember. Although you will see a number of activities listed on the following pages, I caution you to use good judgement and select sparingly. Children will come to dislike literature if we burn them out by expecting them to do too much with it. As you review the activities, think of your own students, their needs and likes, the resources available to you, and the time constraints under which you are working. Select one or perhaps two activities that will work best in your classroom situation. To read a ten minute story and do two weeks of related activities is to take away the excitement and enjoyment of a good book.

I once heard it said that teachers of literature are entrepreneurs who advertise, share, and sell books. I always liked that message, and I encourage you to be a lover and good teacher of children's literature by using books in positive and enriching ways. Remember those meaningful words of Judith O'Malley (1997), "stack the firewood in the form of wonderful books that fan the flame to extend the experience of learning and reading" (p. 3). Some of my favorite pieces of "firewood" can be found on the following pages, and the kid-tested, teacher-approved literature ideas are certain to "fan the flame" of even the most reluctant reader.

Featured Books Listed by Theme

FAMILY AND FRIENDS
Snake Alley Band (Elizabeth Nygaard)
Wanted: Best Friend (A. M. Monson)
Meet Calliope Day (Charles Haddad)
The Fabulous Flying Fandinis (Ingrid Slyder)

YOUR COMMUNITY AND BEYOND
Wish You Were Here: Emily's Guide to the 50 States (Kathleen Krull)
Alphabet City (Stephen Johnson)
How to Make an Apple Pie and See the World (Marjorie Priceman)

OUR COUNTRY'S PAST
The Flag We Love (Pam Munoz Ryan)
Nine for California (Sonia Levitin)
The Wagon Train (Bobbi Kalman)

THE ENVIRONMENT
What's New with Mr. Pizooti (Barbara Kupetz)
Safari (Robert Bateman)
Dear Children of the Earth (Schim Schimmel)
Where Once There Was A Wood (Denise Fleming)

MATH IN DISGUISE
Two of Everything (Lily Hong)
Measuring Penny (Loreen Leedy)
Betcha (Stuart Murphy)
How Big is a Foot? (Rolf Myller)

EXPLORING LANGUAGE AND LETTERS
Martha Blah Blah (Susan Meddaugh)
Tomorrow's Alphabet (George Shannon)
Four Famished Foxes and Fosdyke (Pam Duncan Edwards)
A Stitch in Rhyme (Illustrated by Belinda Downes)
Frindle (Andrew Clement)

SCHOOL AND TEACHERS
Lilly's Purple Plastic Purse (Kevin Henkes)
Teacher from the Black Lagoon (Mike Thaler)
Thank You, Mr. Falker (Patricia Polacco)
Dear Mr. Blueberry (Simon James)

FAIRY AND TALL TALES
Folks Call Me Appleseed John (Andrew Glass)
William the Curious, Knight of the Water Lilies (Charles Santore)
Fanny's Dream (Caralyn Buehner)
Rapunzel, A Happenin' Rap (David Vozar)

JUST FOR THE FUN OF IT
The Fixits (Anne Mazer)
Grandpa's Teeth (Rod Clement)
Mistakes That Worked (Charlotte Foltz Jones)

Figure 6.1
Literature Across the Curriculum Matrix

BOOK TITLES	Reading/ Writing	Oral Language	Math	Science/ Cooking	Social Studies	Art/ Music	HOTS*
Snake Alley Band		•			•	•	•
Wanted: Best Friend	•				•	•	•
Meet Calliope Day	•	•					•
The Fabulous Flying Fandinis	•	•			•	•	•
Wish You Were Here	•				•	•	•
Alphabet City	•				•	•	•
How to Make An Apple Pie and See the World	•	•	•	•	•	•	•
The Flag We Love	•	•			•	•	•
Nine for California	•				•	•	•
The Wagon Train	•	•			•	•	•
What's New with Mr. Pizooti	•	•		•	•	•	•
Safari	•	•	•	•	•	•	•
Dear Children of the Earth		•		•		•	•
Where Once There Was a Wood	•	•		•			•
Two of Everything	•	•	•				•
Measuring Penny	•	•	•				•
Betcha	•	•	•				•
How Big is a Foot?	•	•	•			•	
Martha Blah Blah	•	•					•
Tomorrow's Alphabet	•	•				•	•
Four Famished Foxes and Fosdyke	•	•		•			•
A Stitch in Time	•	•					•
Frindle	•	•		•		•	•
Lilly's Purple Plastic Purse	•	•			•	•	•
Teacher from the Black Lagoon	•	•	•				•
Thank you, Mr. Falker	•	•			•		
Dear Mr. Blueberry	•	•					•
Folks Call Me Appleseed John	•	•				•	•
William the Curious	•	•		•			•
Fanny's Dream	•	•			•	•	•
Rapunzel, A Happenin' Rap	•	•					•
The Fixits	•	•				•	•
Grandpa's Teeth	•	•	•	•			•
Mistakes That Worked	•	•		•	•	•	•

*HOTS = Higher Order Thinking Skills

FAMILY AND FRIENDS
Snake Alley Band
by Elizabeth Nygaard
Illustrated by Betsy Lewin
Doubleday
1998
Ages 4–10

When the smallest member of the Snake Alley Band awakes from a nap, he discovers that his musician friends have disappeared. But, not to worry, for soon enough other musicians arrive wanting to join Snake for a real musical jam. Only Snake refuses them all because he is so used to the sound of his familiar snake band. Will he choose to be without music, or will he discover that something new and different may be the best music of all?

1. Enjoy this story again as a choral reading. Divide your class into 6 groups and give each one of them fun sounds from the book. These include:

    shhh-boom
    chew up chew-up
    pop pop doo wop
    cha-bop, cha-bob, cha-bob
    tweet-tweedle-dee-deet
    ta-toom-ta-toom-toom

    As you retell the story, allow each group to chime in at the appropriate time for a fun and marvelously musical version.

2. Allow your students to create rhythm instruments out of everyday materials. These can include: rubber-bands around a shoe box, a plastic soda bottle partially filled with water, sand blocks (wooden blocks covered with sandpaper), dried beans inside two paper plates stapled together, several different tin cans and a pencil, etc. As the story is re-read, students create their own special sounds for each animal using their rhythm instruments.

3. The message in this story is that we are all different, and different is a good, not a bad, thing. The animals in the newly created Snake Alley Band were all different in the way they looked and the sounds they made, but together they worked together to make beautiful music. Your students have many similarities and differences. We are not all alike! Using the "All About Me" chart (see appendix A), ask your students to color the bottom half of every space that is true about them. They must then find a classmate for whom this is also true and print their name there in the top half. Not only is this a

good way to point out similarities and differences, but a great way to get to know each other early in the school year. The chart can be easily changed to better reflect your age group or even done with pictures rather than words for the youngest of students.

4.   Further explore the notion of similarities and differences within your classroom. Allow each child to create his/her personal Coat of Arms (see appendix A). Begin with a lesson on symmetry as you show children how to fold the paper in half and draw only half of the shape that will (when cut properly) result in a perfectly symmetrical shape. Allow children to divide the Coat of Arms in any way they'd like and to include information about themselves in pictures and word. You may find it helpful to offer some ideas to children to select from such as: favorite food, my family, favorite TV show, famous person I would like to meet, favorite thing I like to do with my family, something I like to do in my free time, my birthday, etc. Students can make a colorful background for their Coat of Arms by using the same "symmetry trick" of folding a piece of large colored paper from the rolls many schools have and drawing a shape one inch larger than the Coat of Arms.

Other Related Books:

Cannon, J. (1993). *Stellaluna*. San Diego: Harcourt Brace.
Eduar, G. (1997). *Jooka saves the day*. New York: Orchard.
Johnston, T. (1995). *The iguana brothers*. New York: Scholastic.
Pryor, B. (1997). *Louie and Dan are friends*. New York: Morrow.

～～

FAMILY AND FRIENDS
Wanted: Best Friend
by A. M. Monson
Illustrated by Lynn Munsinger
Dial Books for Young Readers
1997
Ages 4–9

When Cat and Mouse have a disagreement about a card game, Cat decides it is time for a new friend and posts an ad in the newspaper. Several less than desirable applicants stop by, and it doesn't take Cat long to realize that his old, dear friend is the best friend of all. Soon they are happily playing crazy eights again.

1. What do your students look for as they select a "best friend?" Brainstorm with your class and make a list of the qualities that each of us hopes to find in our friends.

2. Create Wanted Posters on drawing paper or using a computer program that makes borders. Create a variety of different borders and allow children to select the "picture frame" they like best. Each child will need to identify several criteria that he/she considers important for a best friend and list them on the poster. Also, have each child draw a picture of "you and your best friend doing something together." Hang the posters around the room or in a hall display while you enjoy this book and others about friends.

3. Older students might enjoy making a tri-fold brochure to announce qualities of a best friend. Using a 12" x 18" sheet of paper, cut it in half the long way. Each child will then have a 6" x 18" sheet to fold into three parts so it is self-standing. In the center of the tri-fold, students can draw themselves doing something with a best friend and the words "To apply you must be…". On the left section write, "My best friend must…and on the right "My best friend must NOT…".

4. Best friends do many things. Sometimes they even help solve problems. Create an Advice Network in your classroom. As you select the classroom helpers each week be sure to select a classroom advisor known as Dear Gabby. Each week that student is responsible for offering advice to students who submit a problem. Place a Dear Gabby box in a special place in your classroom. Each day during the week, students may deposit problem situations and Dear Gabby must respond in writing by using a clothespin to hang the response on the question box. Students do not sign real names, but fictitious ones. If you first review a Dear Abby column with your students, they will get the idea quickly and enjoy being the one who gives or gets advice. Take this Advice Network one step beyond individual classroom problems to the problem situations found in the books we read. As your class reads and discusses a book, ask children to offer advice to a book character just as Dear Abby would.

5. In the story, Raccoon said, "Raccoon is my name and skateboarding is my game." Discuss what "my game" means and allow each child to complete the sentence to fit his or her interests. (Ex: Barbara is my name and reading is my game.") This will help reinforce how each of us is unique and that all of us have different skills, talents, and abilities.

Other Related Books:

Brown, L. K. & Brown, M. T. (1998). *How to be a friend: A guide to making friends and keeping them.* Boston: Little, Brown.

Carle, E. (1988). *Do you want to be my friend?* New York: Putnam.
Clifford, E. (1996). *Family for sale.* Boston: Houghton Mifflin.
Kellogg, S. (1986). *Best friends.* New York: Dutton.

⁓

FAMILY AND FRIENDS
Meet Calliope Day
by Charles Haddad
Illustrated by Steve Pica
Bantam Doubleday Dell
1998
Ages 7–11

Filled with knee-slapping, laugh-out-loud humor that will tickle your students, this is a great new voice for the middle grade child. Much like the Ramona books filled with daily dilemmas for the heroine, this book shares with the reader Calliope's problems. Kids will identify with this contemporary Dennis the Menace type character's problems and the resourcefulness she uses to solve them.

1. Calliope has a problem when Mrs. Perkins takes her pink fangs. Use the problem-solving chart (see appendix A) to identify some possible solutions and the feasibility of each. The creativity of your students will make this a fun activity!
2. Calliope has surely had several problems, but maybe there is a problem you have had (or a friend you know) which hasn't yet happened to Calliope. Use this problem to create a new chapter in Calliope Day's story. Using the characters from the book (you can add others if you'd like) give Calliope your problem and see how she will solve it. Share your chapter with the class.
3. In this book, Calliope doesn't always agree with her teacher or her mom, but we know both of them are doing their job. What is the job we expect certain people to do. Brainstorm to make a list of jobs (careers). Then allow students to select one to draw and write about. By folding a large sheet of drawing paper in half, students can on one side draw a person in that career and on the other side list some of the things that person should do. A good springboard into Career Week!

Other Related Books:
Duffey, B. (1996). *Hey new kid*! New York: Viking.
Fowler, S. L. (1998). *Albertine the practically perfect*. New York: Greenwillow.

Komaiko, L. (1997). *Annie Bananie, best friend to the end*. New York: Delacorte.

Lowry, L. (1996). *See you around, Sam*! Boston: Houghton Mifflin.

≈≈≈

FAMILY AND FRIENDS
The Fabulous Flying Fandinis
by Ingrid Slyder
Cobblehill Books
1996
Ages 6–11

The Fandini family moves into the neighborhood and at the insistence of his mother, Bobby reluctantly pays them a visit. He is shocked to find this welcoming circus family and their home to be quite unlike anything he has ever seen! Who wouldn't be a little excited yet fearful of such "different" people? Will Bobby accept the differences he sees and overcome his fears even at the cost of looking a little foolish?

1. The Fandini's accomplish normal, everyday tasks in somewhat unusual ways (such as serving pancakes while jumping on a trampoline). Organize your students into small cooperative groups of three to four students. Ask each group to select one everyday household task that either they or their parents routinely do. Brainstorm to think, "How might the Fandini's do this job?" Write a paragraph describing the "unique method" and draw a picture to show one of your group members actually doing the task in this new way.

2. Although different in many ways, the Fandini's worked together as a family helping each other. Students can identify all the members of their immediate family and a job each of them does "for the good of the family." Using the hand pattern (see appendix A), make multiple copies so that the class can share them. Cut 12" x 24" construction paper in half (longways) so that each child has two long (6" x 24") sections. Show children how to fold each piece accordion style so that each section is the width of the hand pattern. Trace the pattern and cut out the hands on the lines leaving the folds at the thumb and pinky uncut. On each of the hands, write one statement describing something family members do to help the house run smoothly. (Examples: My mom buys food for us to eat, My sister feeds the cat every day.)

3. Imagine that you have permission from your parents to redecorate you own bedroom. Think of how you would like it to be and draw a

picture that shows how it will look once the decorating is completed.

4. Why not turn your class onto making a board game called the Fabulous Flying Fandinis. Using a manila folder or piece of oak tag have groups of three or four students create a generic game board that could be used for any content area (math, vocabulary review, spelling practice, etc.). The groups should try to incorporate some of the detailed illustrations of the book and the circus motif into the design of their gameboard. Students may choose to use ideas from other game boards such as go back three spaces, loose one turn, and spin again in conjunction with the content of the Fandini story (Ex: slipped from the trapeze—loose one turn). Don't forget that you need a spinner or dice and playing pieces! Each group should decide what the class will review through this game board and make a deck of cards specific to multiplication facts, spelling words, word definitions, social studies content review, etc. In this way, the game board can be used even when the content changes just by making a different deck of cards. Your students will love being "game makers."

Other Related Books:

Carlson, N.L. (1992). *Arnie and the new kid*. New York: Puffin.

Curtis, J. L. (1998). *Today I feel silly and other moods that make my day*. New York: HarperCollins.

Danzinger, P. (1999). *Amber Brown is feeling blue*. New York: Scholastic.

Mitchell, L. (1999). *Different just like me*. Watertown, MA: Charlesbridge Publishing.

Promimos, J. (1999). *The loudness of Sam*. New York: Harcourt Brace.

Wright, H. N. (1999). *Fears, doubts, blues, and pouts: Stories about handling fear, worry, sadness, and anger*. Colorado Springs, CO: Chariot Victor Publishing.

YOUR COMMUNITY AND BEYOND
Wish You Were Here: Emily's Guide to the 50 States
by Kathleen Krull
Illustrated by Amy Schwartz
Bantam Books
1997
Ages 6 and up

After a whirlwind tour of the United States, Emily and her grandmother record their geographic, cultural, and tourist information in this book which takes the form of a travel diary. Their recap of the trip sets the stage for some facts about state capitals, mottos, famous quotes, and cool trivia facts. All of these interesting tidbits are in a kid-friendly format that even adults will enjoy.

1. Make a classroom scrapbook by allowing each child to select a state (or two). Encourage your students to learn all they can about the state they have chosen and use index cards to create photographs for the scrapbook. Using black papers (or a real scrapbook purchased at any discount store) arrange the photos around the page allowing room for the written narrative to tell about the state and its highlights. You may specify what you want your students to include, such as capital, state motto, state flower, state flag, state bird, etc., or permit them to create their own page including what they found to be important. If you choose to use black construction paper to resemble an old photo album, then use white crayon to make notations under the index card "photos."

2. Become an armchair tourist. Select a state and make a tri-fold brochure, a tourism commercial, a travel poster, or a skit. Let this creative choice be your way to spread the word about all your state has to offer.

3. Many of the cities you will learn about will be large, metropolitan areas. Discuss what it would be like to live right in the heart of a big city. How would your life be different or the same as it is where you now live? Use the left circle of a Venn Diagram to illustrate how life would be in a big city, use the other circle to tell things about your life in a smaller town, and the similarities between your lives should be placed in the area that overlaps.

4. This activity is called "City Slickers" and gives each child the opportunity to become an expert on one major U.S. city. The result is that your class will ultimately become very knowledgeable about major cities throughout the country. Students should brainstorm names of major cities in the United States. Make a list. Each child now selects one which he/she would like to learn more about (discourage children from selecting one with which they are already very familiar). Students begin researching their city. Resources can include school and public library materials as well as information gathered from travel agencies and the local AAA. If your school has Internet capabilities, this is an excellent source of information about various cities. The goal is for each student to become the "expert" on their chosen city. To demonstrate what each has learned, students will create a "city in a box." Do this by gathering a pizza box for each child from your local Pizza Hut (they are sturdy and work best). Children will need to use Popsicle sticks or tongue depressors to

strengthen the lid of the box and keep it upright (open). Use this box with an attached flip up lid to build a diorama of the city you have investigated. Be sure to include items of interest about that city using a variety of materials. On the lid of the box there should be a paragraph briefly describing your city.

Your class can now create their own travel seminar. Invitations can be made so that parents and other classes can visit. As guests walk around your classroom, each of your students is responsible for sharing the highlights about his/her city. Students will love being the "experts" and your guests will be in awe of how knowledgeable they are.

5. Children will enjoy using a large map to plot their cities. Notice the geographical relationship of cities. Research how far it would be to travel from your home to each of these cities. This can be the beginning of all sorts of related math activities for these seasoned travelers!

Other Related Books:

Anno, M. (1998). *Anno's USA*. New York: Paperstar.

Perl, L. (1992). *It happened in America: True stories from the fifty states*. New York: Henry Holt.

Peterson, C. (1996). *Harvest year*. Honesdale, PA: Boyds Mills.

Williams, V. B. (1991). *Stringbean's trip to the shining sea*. New York: Scholastic.

≈≈≈

YOUR COMMUNITY AND BEYOND
Alphabet City
by Stephen Johnson
Viking
1995
Ages 6 and up

Finding letters of the alphabet that are in our world rather than merely on the printed page can be so much fun! This book will show you how to look around you to see the alphabet in the strangest of places.

1. After reading the book, carefully examine the classroom to find letters within the room itself. What can you see?
2. Exploring your city is great anytime of year, but National Geography Awareness Week is the second week in November. Why not use that week to begin with your own school and community and branch

out to explore other major cities in the United States and even the world!

Try to replicate what the author has done. Starting with "A" examine your community for alphabet letters in everyday things. Students report on letters they find and borrow the classroom camera (disposable cameras work well for this activity) to take a picture of that location and the letter depicted. Invite a photographer in to discuss the correct way to use a camera—how close, framing subjects, etc. Create your own *Alphabet World* specific to your community using photographs and written text. *Alphabet World in Reedsville* or *Alphabet World in Lamperstown*. Suggestion: Limit each child to clicking two pictures. You know why!

3. Use magazines to find the letters of the alphabet in pictures. Make similar alphabet books using these magazine clips.

Other Related Books:

Fisher, L. E. (1991). *The ABC exhibit*. New York: Atheneum.

McAnally, K. (1995). *Letters from the canyon*. Grand Canyon, AZ: Grand Canyon Association.

Paulsen, G. (1997). *Work song*. San Diego: Harcourt Brace.

Tamar, E. (1996). *The garden of happiness*. San Diego: Harcourt Brace.

Walker, N., & Kalman, B. D. (1997). *Community helpers from A to Z*. New York: Crabtree.

～

YOUR COMMUNITY AND BEYOND
How to Make an Apple Pie and See the World
by Marjorie Pricemam
Random House
1994
Ages 4–10

Baking a pie is always fun, but what do you do if the store is closed and you need ingredients? Why of course, you travel the world to find them. From Italy to England, France to Sri Lanka, Jamaica to Vermont—this apple pie takes readers around the globe.

1. How do you make an apple pie (providing you have all the ingredients)? Ask children to tell you the steps to making a pie (as described in the story). After the class has identified the major steps in the correct sequential order, let each child (or two children working together) illustrate one step on a 4" x 6" index card. On the reverse

side of the card, students should use words to describe the step. Now place all cards into a self-closing plastic storage bag and you have a ready-made sequencing activity. Your students can spread them out and arrange them in sequential order.

2. Play "Around the World with _____" Game. This can be used to review vocabulary words, color or number words, math facts, or any content your students could use a little extra practice with. Simply enlarge the reproducible "world" (see appendix A). Use the apple pattern to reproduce so that color words, math facts, vocabulary words, etc., can be printed on each apple. Students reach in the "apple basket" to select an apple. If they can correctly read, solve, or answer what is written on the apple, they may place it around the world. If not, it goes back into the basket. The game is finished when the players get the apples completely around the world.

3. Make a class cookbook as a family gift. Ask each family to send in one recipe they especially enjoy. Collect these and make a classroom cookbook. Children will love to see their name and that of their family on the pages of the book.

4. Make your own apple pie pizza! Using store bought pizza shells and canned apples for pie making, create your own delicious treat.

5. Encourage your students to investigate the countries found in this book. Provide a grid to guide their investigation (see appendix A). Working in groups and using a variety of resources in your classroom or library see which team can correctly locate all the answers!

Other Related Books:

Cave, K. (1999). *W is for world: Around the world ABC.* (1999). New York: Silver Burdett Press.

Gordon, P., & Snow, R. (1999). *Kids learn America.* Charlotte, VT: Williamson Publishing.

Schuett, S. (1997). *Somewhere in the world right now.* Montclair, New Jersey: Dragonfly.

Yourkins, A. (1999). *The alphabet atlas.* Oxfordshire, England: Winslow Press.

OUR COUNTRY'S PAST
The Flag We Love
by Pam Munoz Ryan
Illustrated by Ralph Masiello
Charlesbridge Publishers
1996
Ages 6 and up

A tribute to the American flag, helping the reader understand how the flag was first made and the many and various ways in which it has been used over the years. A combination of historical information with prose and verse set among oil paintings, this book will serve as a helpful resource for teachers.

1. Using this book, as well as other resources, collect flag trivia. Using a string hung at an angle from ceiling to floor, your class can make their own collection of patriotic facts about the American flag. Precut red and white strips of paper approximately 3" x 12". Each time a child learns a new "flag fact" they can use a pinch clothespin to hang it on the string. Blue stars cut from paper can be used to number and identify the contributor. See how many facts you can learn about the American flag. Can you find 50—one for each of the 50 states?

2. Have a Flag Trivia Scavenger Hunt. Prepare a reading area of the room. Allow your students to decorate it in red, white, and blue streamers and patriotic items. During free time, students can visit the All American Reading Corner and attempt to complete the Flag Trivia Scavenger Hunt. Each teacher can decide the actual terms of the hunt. The books available in your All American Reading Corner may determine this. The Scavenger Hunt sheet should have three columns. Who will be the first to accurately find all the flag trivia?

Flag Fact	Book Where You Found It	Page Number
1. Who made the first American Flag?		
2. How is the flag used in the Olympic Games?		
3. Is a flag ever used at a funeral? How?		
4. When are flags placed at half-staff?		

3.   There are a number of points of flag etiquette we should know. Divide your class into eight groups so that each group can explore one area of flag etiquette. These include:

Displaying the flag

Hanging the flag outdoors

Hanging the flag indoors

Raising and lowering the flag

Carrying the flag

Saluting the flag

Caring for the flag

Uses of the flag—What is permitted and prohibited

Each group should research these topics and share their information with the class. They should also use a small flag to demonstrate flag etiquette.

Other Related Books:

Burleigh, R. (1997). *Who said that? Famous Americans speak*. New York: Henry Holt.

Quiri, P. R. (1998). *The American flag (true books)*. San Francisco: Children's Press.

Spier, P. (1991). *We the people: The Constitution of the United States of America*. New York: Doubleday.

Spier, P. (1992). *The starspangled banner*. New York: Yearling.

Swanson, J. (1991). *I pledge allegiance*. Minneapolis, MN: Carolrhoda.

OUR COUNTRY'S PAST
Nine for California
by Sonia Levitin
Illustrated by Cat Bowman Smith
Orchard Books
1996
Ages 6 and up

Pa is out west in California searching for gold. When he writes asking for the family to join him, *everyone* is excited! As they set off on their 21 day stagecoach journey, the other three adult passengers wonder how Mama will keep the five children happy on this long trip using only what she has packed in her sack.

1. Everyone loves a vacation! Sometimes getting there is the best, or worst, part. Ask your students to imagine they are traveling for 21 days to California. In the story, Mama carefully planned things to fill her bag. Allow your students to plan what they would take for the long trip and why they would choose these items. Remember…it must all fit in one duffel bag!

2. Every class needs a travel center. If your students could take a trip far away, where would they go? Using a variety of maps, an atlas, travel brochures, and other resources, allow them to plan the trip realistically using factual and accurate information (if driving in a car, it would take more than a day or two to get to California from Pennsylvania). How would they get there (plane, boat, car, bus, train, or a combination of ways)? What sites would they stop and see along the way? How long will the trip take? Depending upon the age/grade level, this activity can be as simple or as involved as you would like.

3. This story was set during the mid 1800s Gold Rush. Encourage students to imagine they were traveling by car for 21 days, what events might occur to make the trip more interesting? Then ask your students to rewrite the story to reflect more modern problems and settings. They can then write and illustrate their own book about nine people going to California. What would a modern day mother take with her on such a trip to help keep everyone happy?

Other Related Books:

Ackerman, K. (1998). *Araminta's paint box*. New York: Aladdin.

Blos, J. (1996). *Nellie Bly's monkey*. New York: Morrow.

Brown, D. (1997). *Alice Ramsey's grand adventure*. Boston: Houghton Mifflin.

Geriard, R. (1996). *Wagon's west!* New York: Farrar Straus & Giroux.

Johnston, T. (1996). *How many miles to Jacksonville?* New York: Putnam.

Rand, G. (1997). *Baby in a basket*. New York: Cobblehill.

Sanders, S. R. (1989). *Aurora means dawn*. New York: Simon & Schuster.

Tunnel, M. O. (1997). *Mailing May*. New York: Greenwillow.

Turner, A. (1997). *Mississippi mud: Three prairie journals*. New York: HarperCollins.

OUR COUNTRY'S PAST
The Wagon Train
by Bobbi Kalman
Crabtree Publishers
1998
Ages 5–9

Pioneers, brimming with hopes and dreams, were the first immigrants to the west as they loaded up their wagons and headed across the frontier searching for a new life. Discover the routes they took, the hardships they endured, what they ate, and all about their wagons and their dangerous journey in this fact filled book.

1. Many of the idiomatic expressions we use today actually originated in the 1800s. Help students appreciate the origin of such figurative language by discussing some popular idioms of the day and how they began (many more can be found in Marvin Terban's *The Scholastic Book of Idioms*, 1996). Some idioms that began during the westward movement are:

    "Fix your wagon" means to get even with someone, and it began during the time of covered wagons. To fix means to take revenge.

    "One horse town" is an expression that means a dull place. It began when there were more horses around than people. If you visited a town that had only one horse, it must have been pretty small and dull.

    "Quick on the draw" means to be very alert. Long ago, cowboys were judged on how quickly they could get their pistols out of their holster to shoot.

    "Shoe on the other foot" means to switch places or situations with another person. Until the 1800s no one was concerned about wearing a certain shoe on a certain foot. Left or right—it didn't matter. You could wear either shoe on either foot. After you wore a shoe on one foot for awhile, it would begin to take on the shape (conform) to that foot's shape. If you accidentally put the shoe on the wrong foot, it felt strange, like you would feel if a situation were switched.

2. Create a cinquain poem about pioneer life. Explain to your student poets the structure of this seven-line contrast poem. Have students brainstorm a list of nouns, verbs, and adjectives, relating to the westward movement and pioneer life. Have each student select one noun and follow the cinquain formula to create their formula poems. Display these poems on a bulletin board or hall display called "Westward Ho—Poetry Ho."

Line 1	one word	a noun for the title
Line 2	two words	adjectives describing the title
Line 3	three words	expressing action relating to the title
Line 4	four words	expressing feeling about the title word
Line 5	one word	either repeating the title or closely related to the title

3. Even long ago, travelers used maps to find their way. Although not as sophisticated as today, these maps showed landforms (rivers, mountains, etc.) and directions of the compass rose. Using the coordinates on the grid (see appendix A) mark the points where some of the landforms and settings of the book take place. Then give your partner an empty grid and as you call out coordinates (Example: the forest is at D4), the partner will try to plot these points with only that information. Compare maps. They should be the same!

4. Although none of our living relatives experienced the westward movement first-hand, we do know that life in the past (during our parents and grandparents days) was quite different. Ask each child to select an older family member or friend and identify between three and seven questions the student would like to ask that might demonstrate how life has changed. Have students make arrangements to interview that person, writing down the answers to the selected questions. You might want to help students formulate questions such as:

   - What are some modern conveniences that I use that you did not have as a child? Which ones were very different?
   - What were some of your favorite family activities?
   - Where did you live as a child? How has that place changed since you lived there?
   - What were some of your favorite games or pastimes as a child?

Other Related Books:

Bunting, E. (1995). *Dandelions*. New York: Harcourt Brace.

Cushman, K. (1996). *The ballad of Lucy Whipple*. New York: Houghton Mifflin.

Kroll, S. (1996). *Pony express*. New York: Scholastic.

Turner, A. W. (1997). *Mississippi mud: Three prairie journals*. New York: HarperCollins.

THE ENVIRONMENT
What's New with Mr. Pizooti?
by Barbara N. Kupetz
Perfection Learning
1997
Ages 7–10

Louie Pizooti is a collector—his yard and his house are filled with things others have thrown away. Louie believes there is a need to use and reuse everything we can. He believes in recycling! When his neighbor, Matt, needs some help in finding a project for the Science Fair at school, Louie is there to help. In the end, everyone has learned a powerful lesson about the three R's of trash and about life.

1. As a part of your theme regarding the environment and environmental concerns, urge your students to consider ways we can work together to make the community and the school a better and more "environmentally correct" place.

2. Working in small groups, students can identify a focus area (downtown park, recreation center, school playground, etc.) that is frequented by classmates and townspeople. They can write a script as well as edit, direct, and tape both video and audio segments of a public service announcement advocating community care and clean-up.

    The video segments of public service announcements can be viewed by classrooms around the school. The audio segments can be included as part of the broadcasting day on the local radio station. You'd be surprised how willing community organizations such as radio stations will be to feature a 30 second segment produced by children. Your children (and their families) will be excited to hear their environmental messages. As they learn the value of community and the cooperative spirit, they will see that what they do does have an impact and can create a difference.

Other Related Books:

Delton, J. (1992). *Trash bash*. New York: Yearling.

Disalvo-Ryan, D. (1994). *City green*. New York: Morrow.

Leedy, L. (1991). *The great trash bash*. New York: Holiday.

Martin, J. B. (1997). *The green truck garden giveaway: A neighborhood story and almanac*. New York: Simon & Schuster.

Thompson, C. (1997). *The paper bag prince*. Madison, WI: Demco Media.

THE ENVIRONMENT
Safari
by Robert Bateman
Little, Brown & Company
1998
Ages 9 and up

A wonderful wildlife artist, Robert Bateman, takes the young reader on a trip to Africa to observe different animals (many endangered species) and learn something about their behavior.

1. Use this book as a springboard to learning about endangered species around the world. Explore this by bringing other resources to your classroom. As a whole class activity, make a list of endangered animals around the world.

2. Use the list created in the above activity to make a bar graph demonstrating the homes of these animals. On the vertical axis list the continents. Beside each continent, place an index card with the drawing of each endangered species and its name. Use this pictorial representation to show not only the animals in danger, but also the continents most affected by the endangerment of animals.

Continent	1	2	3	4	5	6	7
North America							
South America							
Africa							
Asia							
Australia							
Antarctica							
Europe							

3. Take part in an in-depth study of selected endangered animals. Show your findings by making an Animal Wheel. Starting with a picture or drawing of the animal in the center, draw concentric circles (each

about two inches larger) to form a visual format for sharing information. Include such facts as home continent, natural habitat, food, how it finds food, enemies, the life cycle, care for young, and other interesting facts.

4. Many people travel around the world to see animals that are in danger of extinction. Become the owner of a tour guide business in any continent you choose. Prepare a brochure to describe the service you provide. Where will you take your clients, how will you get them there, how do you provide for their safety, what will they see, how should they dress, what will this cost, and when is this available? Use what you know about the animal you are preparing to see to decide how your tour will be designed. For instance, if you know that in the heat of the afternoon, one of the best places to find an elephant is at a watering hole or a river as they try to cool down, use that information in your planning.

Other Related Books:

Arnold, C. (1997). *African animals*. New York: Morrow.

Curtis, P. (1997). *Animals you never even heard of*. San Francisco: Sierra Club.

Krasemann, S. J. & Bach, B. (1998). *African wildlife: A photographic safari*. Minocqua, WI: North Word.

Lasky, K. (1997). *The most beautiful roof in the world: Exploring the rainforest canopy*. San Diego: Harcourt.

~~~

THE ENVIRONMENT
Dear Children of the Earth
by Schim Schimmel
North Word Press
1994
Ages 7 and up

Mother Earth writes a letter to all the children who live on the planet, urging them to take care of the environment.

1. Mother Earth knows that each and every one of us is unique. Allow students to describe what is unique or special about them.

2. Help students become more familiar with the effects of environmental problems by examining food chains. In small groups, they may choose one animal to become extinct. Have them discover what happens to the other animals as a result, as well as the extinction's effect

on humans. This can also be done with polluted environments such as clean oceans, forest destruction, lakes, etc.

3. Mother Earth asks us to let people know what we can do to take care of each other. Discuss with your class what can be done locally and on a more global level. Design flyers and posters (or even a web site) to share this information with others.

4. If you have Internet access, link with another class around the world. Find out what environmental concerns they have and how they compare to your students' ideas.

Other Related Books:

Asch, F. (1994). *The earth and I*. New York: Harcourt Brace.

Baker, J. (1991). *Window*. New York: Penguin.

Bosveld, J. (1997). *While a tree was growing*. New York: Workman.

Bouchard, D. (1990). *The elders are watching*. Tofino, BC, Canada: Eagle Dancer Enterprises.

Brown, R. (1991). *The world that Jack built*. New York: Dutton.

Cherry, L. (1990). *The great kapok tree: A tale of the Amazon rain forest*. San Diego: Harcourt Brace.

Cowcher, H. (1988). *Rain forest*. New York: Farrar Straus & Giroux.

Ryder, J. (1996). *Earthdance*. New York: Henry Holt.

Waldman, N. (1997). *The neverending greeness*. New York: Morrow.

⤢

THE ENVIRONMENT
Where Once There Was a Wood
by Denise Fleming
Henry Holt
1996
Ages 4–8

Visit the natural world with pheasants, red fox, raccoons, horned owls, and other animals brought to life in the ecological tribute to our disappearing wildlife. It is a celebration of earth and its creatures that shows us the simple yet significant ways we can help in our own backyard.

1. Children can create their own "Flemingesque" creations with torn paper to replicate her colorful illustrations. NO SCISSORS ALLOWED! Encourage children to select a woodland animal and create it in its natural habitat through the tearing of construction paper and pasting it to a 9" x 12" paper. You might instead try a class mural all done with torn paper.

2. Denise Fleming using uncommon vocabulary in her text such as roosted, unfurled, and rummaged. Encourage children to identify all those words that are not a part of their everyday language. Make a "word hanging" by cutting long pieces of butcher paper no wider than 12 inches. Once children identify and write the many words that are new to them, hang this lengthy list from a skirt or pants hanger. This can be hung from a high out of the way place in the room and not take up valuable chalkboard or bulletin board space. The hanger can later be used for other displays by simply switching the piece of paper.
3. Using the alphabet as a guide, can your students create the ABCs of attracting and preserving wildlife? A is for _____, B is for _____. This can be done in the form of a class book or a hall display with posters that goes throughout the school. Both younger and older students will be looking for the next letter hoping to figure out what the wildlife tip might be!

Other Related Books:

Cherry, L. (1992). *A river ran wild*. New York: Harcourt Brace.
Cooney, B. (1982). *Miss Rumphius*. New York: Viking Press.
Disalvo-Ryan, D. (1994). *City green*. New York: William Morrow.
Gibbons, G. (1997). *Nature's green umbrella*. New York: Mulberry.
Ryder, J. (1996). *Earthdance*. New York: Herny Holt & Company.
Wright, A. *Will we miss them? Endangered species*. Watertown, MA: Charlesbridge Publishing.
Yolen J. (1993). *Welcome to the greenhouse*. New York: Putnam.

⁓

MATH IN DISGUISE
Two of Everything
by Lily Toy Hong
Albert Whitman & Company
1993
Ages 6–10

In this amusing Chinese folktale, an elderly couple digs up a large, old brass pot in their field and discover it is magic. Mr. Haktak drops in his purse with five coins and, behold, a second purse with five coins appears. The pot doubles whatever is placed inside it! But one day, Mrs. Haktak falls in and the family learns that not everything in life is best doubled!

1. This book lends itself well to math and the concept of "doubling" for younger audiences and the larger idea of "functions" for older audiences. With younger audiences: After reading the book, review the items that were put in the pot and what resulted in the magical doubling. Make a chart to show these items. Continue by making up problems of your own—If seven pencils fell into the pot, how many would come out of the pot? If 33 candies fell into the pot, how many would come out of the pot? These story problems should reflect the math ability of the students with whom you are working. Allow your students to create some problems of their own to try to stump the class. Take this one step further by comparing the doubling process as multiplication by two. How would we write each of these stories as a multiplication problem?

2. With older audiences, use this story to introduce the concept of "function." Tell students, "This is a magical pot and whatever number goes into the pot determines the number that will come out of the pot." Draw a chart and begin to place numbers on the chart.

IN	OUT
4	8
6	12
10	20

Can they figure out the magic function of the pot? Continue to change the game making each a bit more difficult.

These can get as complicated as appropriate for your students. You may even want to include multiple operations such as 4 + 3 or plus 5 minus 1. Students love having the chance to make magic of their own to stump others. What is magical about the numbers I have used below?

IN	OUT
4 + 3 - 5 + 6	8
13 - 4 + 7 - 2	14

Other Related Books:

Anno, M. (1983). *Anno's mysterious multiplying jar*. New York: Putnam.

Demi (1997). *One grain of rice: A mathematical folktale*. New York: Scholastic.

Hutchins, P. (1989). *The doorbell rang*. New York: Mulberry.

Leedy, L. (1996). *2 x 2 = Boo: A set of spooky multiplication stories*. New York: Holiday.

Neuschwander, C., & Burns, M. (1998). *Amanda Bean's amazing dream*. New York: Scholastic.

Pinczes, E. J. (1993). *One hundred hungry ants*. Boston: Houghton Mifflin.

Pinczes, E. J. (1995). *A remainder of one*. Boston: Houghton Mifflin.

Pinczes, E. J. (1996). *Arctic five arrive*. New York: Scholastic.

MATH IN DISGUISE
Measuring Penny
by Loreen Leedy
Henry Holt and Company
1997
Ages 6–10

Lisa has a math assignment—she has to measure something in several different ways. She needs to include standard and non-standard units, but what will she measure? Why not Penny, her dog! Through this assignment, Lisa learns not only a lot about her dog, but also learns a great deal about measuring and has lots of fun, too!

1. When most children hear the word measurement, they think of linear units such as inch, foot, yard, etc. Brainstorm with your class to discover the many different ways we can measure and some of the units we might use. These could include linear measurement (inch, yard, mile, foot), volume measurement (cup, gallon, teaspoon, liter), time measurement (hour, minute, day, week, month, year, century), weight measurement (pound, ounce, ton), temperature measurement (degrees), or money (dollars, cents).

2. Select some common object that is standard (for instance the math book the students are currently using). After reading the story, allow students to choose any of the non-standard units used in the text (for instance, dog biscuits) and measure the object. Now find three other unusual non-standard units you could bring to class and demonstrate measuring with these.

    When the author discusses measurement using units of time, she makes a daily schedule for Penny. Have children create their own school day schedule beginning with waking up and ending with going home. Be sure to include the times when things happen. For instance,

7:00 Wake up
7:00–7:30 Get dressed
7:30–7:40 Eat breakfast
7:47–Walk to bus

3. Think of something that occupies a good deal of your time each day (not counting school). Maybe playing with friends, involvement in a club or team, watching TV, music lessons, etc. Create a chart that allows you to record the minutes each day you are engaged in this activity. Add up your minutes of involvement and collaborate with class members to create a class graph. The same can be done with calculating money spent, amount of milk you drink, etc.

Other Related Books:

Glass, J. (1998). *The fly on the ceiling: A math myth.* New York: Scholastic.
Hightower, S. (1997). *Twelve snails to one lizard: A tale of mischief and measurement.* New York: Simon & Schuster.
Murphy, S. J. (1999). *Super sand castle Saturday (math start).* New York: HarperCollins.
Myller, R. (1991). *How big is a foot?* New York: Yearling.

⌇

MATH IN DISGUISE
Betcha!
by Stuart J. Murphy
HarperCollins Publishers
1997
Ages 8–10

Two friends begin with a "count the jelly bean contest" and continue to estimate just about everything from people on the bus to the cost of the toys in a store window. As they estimate, they describe the way in which they do it, making this book a great one for understanding the concept.

1. Discuss other real life situations that utilize estimation from ordering pizza for the whole class to deciding how many math problems you could do in 15 minutes. How would you go about solving these estimation questions?

2. Make up your own "Betcha" game by selecting something that is hard to count such as students in the school, pretzel sticks in a box, tiles on the hall floor. What strategies can we use to make these estimates? Check your estimates with the real answers you get from counting.

3. Using the grocery ads in the Saturday newspaper, estimate the cost of a meal for your family. Can you use a menu from a local restaurant and estimate the cost of your family eating out?
   Use the calculator to get the exact answer. Was your estimate close?

4. Create An Estimation Fair. Each student is responsible to create one estimation activity for the fair. They should prepare all the rules, all the materials for the contest, and, of course, should have counted so they know in advance the exact answer. Students will use their estimating skills to attempt to get as many points as possible at the fair. One point is awarded to the person who gets the closest through his/her estimation skills, and at the end of the fair small prizes can be awarded.

Other Related Books:

Clement, R. (1991). *Counting on Frank*. Milwaukee, WI: Gareth Stevens.

Pittman, H. (1994). *Counting Jennie*. Minneapolis, MN: Lerner.

Schwartz, D. M. (1993). *How much is a million?* New York: Mulberry.

MATH IN DISGUISE
How Big is a Foot?
by Rolf Myller
Bantam Doubleday Dell Books
1990
Ages 5–9

The king wants to give the queen something special for her birthday, but she has just about everything except a bed. The problem is that no one in the kingdom knows the answer to the important question, "How big is a bed?" because beds had not yet been invented! With the queen's birthday only a few days away, how can the king know what size the bed should be?

1. Introduce the concept of nonstandard measurement by brainstorming ways in which we could measure an object if rulers (tape mea-

sures, etc.) had not been invented. After composing a list of possible solutions to this dilemma, select several options that are available to the class and set off on measuring objects around the room. Did students get the same or different answers? Discuss why? Which measurements were most accurate? Which ways of measuring are best suited for certain objects and why (You wouldn't want to measure the classroom by the width of your pinky would you?).

2. Give each student an object that is identical or a duplicated picture of the same object. Try to measure that object using ten different non-standard measurements. Use the chart in appendix A to record your different measurements.

3. When it comes to measurement using standard units, students are often confused about just "what equals what" such as 12 inches equals one foot. If your students are having some difficulty with this, help them by creating Measurement Creatures to clear things up. Students can work in small groups or this can be done as a whole class project. Using the basic shapes of squares, circles, and rectangles, create a large body shape out of chart paper or poster board. Label the largest body part as a large unit of measurement (linear, capacity, weight, or time). For example:

    one yard (torso) = three feet (limbs)

    one foot (limbs) = 12 inches (hands or feet)

    As you can see, each Measurement Creature will be different and uniquely helpful as your students try to make conversions between units of measurement. These student-made Measurement Creatures will not only brighten your room, but also help your students as they tackle measurement problems.

Other Related Books:

Hightower, S. (1997). *Twelve snails to one lizard: A Tale of mischief and measurement*. New York: Simon & Schuster.

Murphy, S. J. (1999). *Room for Ripley*. New York: HarperCollins.

Rex, M. (1997). *The fattest, tallest, biggest snowman ever*. New York: Cartwheel.

EXPLORING LANGUAGE AND LETTERS
Martha Blah Blah
by Susan Meddaugh
Houghton Mifflin
1996
Ages 5–9

When Helen feeds her dog alphabet soup, the letters go to her brain instead of her stomach—the result is Martha becomes a talking dog! However, one day the soup company decides to eliminate some of the letters in the soup. What will happen now when Martha has a bowl of alphabet soup and realizes (as she tries to talk) that she makes no sense? Will Martha stop being the talking dog we all love or will she solve the mystery of the missing alphabet letters?

1. Using the scrambled words that Martha now speaks, challenge your class to discover which alphabet letters have been eliminated by the soup company. Working in teams, see who can discover all the missing letters first.

2. Continuing with the idea of missing letters, give your class a list of any thirteen letters. This can be a-m, n-z or any mix of thirteen letters. Kids also love to reach in a paper bag and randomly select the 13 letters their team will use. With the given letters, what words can each team build? Can anyone build a three letter word? A four letter word? A five or six or seven letter word? What is the longest word anyone can build?

3. Connect the story of Martha with the weekly spelling words. Play a "Wheel of Fortune" type game. Using 7 sheets of construction paper fold each into four sections and cut into 28, 4 1/2 by 6 inch cards (you'll only need 26). On each card print a letter of the alphabet. Stand each letter on the chalk tray for the class to see. Pre-select spelling words or for a real challenge use sentences containing spelling words. Draw dashes on the chalkboard for each letter in each word. This is when you become Vanna White (even if only for Spelling class), and as the students select a letter, you turn over the card to show it has been used and fill in all the letters where they belong. The game can become more sophisticated with certain point values for certain letters to give players "cash" winnings, buying vowels, or teams playing teams. You decide or allow your children to become even more creative. This will add lots of excitement to a usually routine spelling list!

4. Use Alphabets® breakfast cereal to provide a dish of food for Martha. Give a handful to each child. How many REAL words can you build with the letters you have received. Don't eat the evidence until your

words are counted! Integrate math by giving a point values to certain consonants and a different value to each vowel. How many points did you earn for the word you have built?

Other Related Books:

Cahoon, H. (1999). *Word play ABC*. New York: Walker & Co.
Falwell, C. (1997). *Word wizard*. New York: Clarion.
Wood, A. (1996). *Bright and early Thursday evening: A tangled tale*. San Diego: Harcourt Brace.

≈≫

EXPLORING LANGUAGE AND LETTERS
Tomorrow's Alphabet
by George Shannon
Illustrated by Donald Crews
Greenwillow
1996
Ages 6 and up

This is not a book for those learning the ABCs, but for those who know the alphabet well enough that they can play with it! Using the 26 letters of the alphabet, you must be able to think to the future to describe what will be.

1. This serves as a wonderful pattern book and really prompts individual thinking. It can successfully be used by children ages 6–12. After children read or hear the story, they quickly catch on to the pattern the book presents. Children may create their own *Tomorrow's Alphabet* book or each child might take one letter and collaborate to make a class book. What you will find is that students (even the most reluctant readers and typically uninterested children) will really THINK to find a way to trick someone. Students must think of something that begins with a specific letter and then think of what it will become such as "S is for seed—tomorrow's apple."

2. You could really encourage creativity and thinking by making another book called *Yesterday's Alphabet*. It is equally as challenging as students must think to the past. What might this object have been previously?

    D is for dog—yesterday's puppy.
    C is for canal—yesterday's aqueduct.
    A is for ashes—yesterday's campfire.
    C is for chicken—yesterday's egg.

Other Related Books:

Bourke, L. (1995). *Eye spy: A book of alphabet puzzles*. San Francisco, CA: Chronicle.

Elting, M. (1980). *Q is for duck: An alphabet guessing game*. Boston: Houghton Mifflin.

Viorst, J. (1997). *Alphabet from Z to A: (With much confusion on the way)*. New York: Aladdin.

EXPLORING LANGUAGE AND LETTERS
Four Famished Foxes and Fosdyke
by Pamela Duncan Edwards
HarperCollins
1995
Ages 7 and up

A ferocious fracas erupted in the farmyard when four foxes were caught filching fowl. The foxes were famished and desperate for food. Fortunately, their brother Fosdyke who enjoys fried figs, fennel soup, French bread, and fudge fixed a fabulous feast.

1. Capitalize on the letter used in this story, "F" and all 25 other letters, too! Working in cooperative groups, write a sentence using as many "F" words as you can. Examine Graeme Base's beautiful book, *Animalia*, which follows this pattern. Now create an alphabet book of your own with each student contributing an alliterative sentence focusing on one letter. For instance, "An angry anteater had an adventure at the airport." Illustrate your sentence and include pictures of other "a" words (airplane, ant, abacus, apple, alphabet, antique, angel, alligator, etc., on that page). Students may use their dictionaries to find additional words to include. Assemble pages for each letter of the alphabet and create your own class book. An answer key in the back of the book will identify all the words beginning with each letter, and they must be spelled correctly (dictionary skills again)! Groups will challenge other groups, "Can you find 25 words on our page beginning with the letter "D" ?
2. Before reading the story, how many foods beginning with "f" can you list? Bring some of the more unusual ones to class for a tasting party. Have you ever tried a fig? fondue? etc.
3. Select another letter of the alphabet and create a story using that letter. Students must select character names, identify the setting, plan

the plot, climax, and ending all centering around the use of the letter selected.

4. Find other tongue twisters which challenge us because of the alliteration (use of the same beginning consonant sound). Collect these and have a Tongue Twister Contest. Who can say it the fastest and the clearest? Use a stop watch to record each participants time. Find the average time, the difference between two different times, or create any number of math problems from your data.

Other Related Books:

Base, G. (1996). *Animalia*. New York: Puffin.

Cyrus, K. (1997). *Tangle town*. New York: Farrar Straus & Giroux.

Edwards, P. D. (1997). *Dinorella: A prehistoric fairy tale*. New York: Scholastic.

Grover, M. (1997). *The accidental zucchini : An unexpected alphabet*. San Diego: Harcourt Brace.

Jonas, A. (1997). *Watch William walk*. New York: Greenwillow.

Melmed, L. K. (1996). *The marvelous market on mermaid*. New York: Lothrop, Lee, & Shepard.

EXPLORING LANGUAGE AND LETTERS
A Stitch in Rhyme (A Nursery Rhyme Sampler)
Illustrated by Belinda Downes
Alfred A. Knopf
1996
Ages 9 and up

A wonderfully familiar classic for all ages but with the added beauty of a talented artist trained in textiles. The beautifully stitched pictures of Jack and Jill, Humpty Dumpty, Old King Cole, and nearly 50 others make this book quite distinctive.

1. Mother Goose rhymes are a wonderful vehicle for problem solving and writing because often the characters we have come to know so well have a problem which is left unresolved or unsatisfactorily resolved. Consider Little Miss Muffet who at the end of her rhyme has simply run away! And consider Peter Peter Pumpkin Eater—there must be a better solution than that! Couldn't there be a variety of other ways that tale could end? Any nursery rhyme book will do. Let your class first identify the problem of a selected nursery rhyme and then propose to solve this problem following the rhyming pat-

tern presented. Encourage your class to revisit the nursery rhymes of their past via a problem solving approach.

Here's one example of a fourth grade version of a nursery rhyme solution after applying some problem solving strategies and imagination.

Nursery Rhyme	Problem
Jack and Jill	They fell
Peter, Peter, Pumpkin Eater	Left his wife in the pumpkin shell
Humpty Dumpty	Humpty took a dive
Wee Willie Winkie	Running around half dressed

Jack and Jill went up the hill
To get a pail of water.
Jack fell down and broke his crown
And Jill came tumbling after.

Jill got up and brushed the dust
From her shoes and dress and head.
She left Jack there for he seemed not to care
And went directly home to bed.

The very next day Jill proudly did say,
"Jack, we have to stop dating
For I'd like to be with a guy who can see
Not one whose vision is fading."

Other Related Books:

French, V. (1995). *Once upon a time*. Cambridge, MA: Candlewick Press.

Garner, J. F. (1995). *Once upon a more enlightened time : More politically correct bedtime stories*. New York: Simon & Schuster.

Krensky, S. (1995). *The 3 blind mice mystery*. New York: Yearling.

EXPLORING LANGUAGE AND LETTERS
Frindle
by Andrew Clements
Illustrated by Brian Selznick
Simon & Schuster
1996
Ages 9 and up

Nick is a clever 10 year old who decides to torment his teacher by creating a new word for pen ("frindle") and having all of his classmates, then the school, the community, and even the nation begin to use it. From that point on, the war of the words begins and a series of comical events begins. Students will absolutely love Nick, a charming trouble-maker!

1. As Mrs. Granger's students get to know her, a good deal of what they come to believe about her comes from observing her gestures, her eye contact, and her facial expressions. Help your students better understand the use of good observation and the notion of making inferences. Assist each student in secretly selecting another classmate's name. That is the person they will observe for two days, taking notes on what they observe. What can you infer about that person? After the exercise, students will reveal their observational partner and their inferences.

2. Nick quickly becomes a famous person in this book as a result of his ingenuity. His life changes and his actions and behavior seem always to be watched. Ask students to identify other famous people who are constantly watched by the public and their adoring fans. Using the format of an acrostic poem (name poem), students should vertically write the first and last name of this famous person. For each letter in that persons name, students should write a word or phrase that describes the person. Display these creations, and discuss the role and obligations of famous people with your class. How do they feel about the notion of "Role models" or "heroes"?

3. How creative and inventive can your students be? Tap into their creativity by asking them to take a word they often use, and substituting it with another "new" word. Now the fun begins. They must remember to use the new word every time they speak or write for the entire day. Can they do it? In order to better follow their success, students should write the "old" word they are no longer going to use on an index card and wear that taped or pinned to their shirt. If a classmate hears them say that word, they've been tricked and must put a tally on their card. At the end of the day, count and chart the tallies. Who was the most careful speaker of the day? Follow up by

creating a class dictionary with the new words. Remember alphabetical order, pronunciation keys, clearly understood illustrations, and good definitions do matter here.

4. The ability to use context clues is an important reading strategy. Reinforce this through this simple activity called, "previously known as…" Your students should select one noun and one verb. Now, do what Nick did in the book; change that word to another word that is nothing like the original one in sound or spelling. The only way in which you will be able to help your classmates know what the word means is through the context clues you offer when you use it in a sentence. Each student should write a well constructed, context-rich sentence for each word selected on a strip of paper and place it in a basket or bag. Divide your class into teams and begin the game. Each time a team can correctly identify what the new word previously was, the team gets a point.

Other Related Books:

Agee, J. (1999). *Sit on a potato pan, Otis!: More palindromes*. New York: Farrar Straus & Giroux.

Clements, A. (1997). *Double trouble in Walla Walla*. Brookfield, CT: Millbrook Press.

Gwynne, F. (1988). *A chocolate moose for dinner*. New York: Aladdin Paperbacks.

Juster, N. (1998). *As silly as bee's knees, as busy as bees: An astounding assortment of similes*. New York: Beech Tree Books.

Pilkey, D. (1994). *Dog breath*. New York: Scholastic.

Terban, M. (1988). *The dove dove: Funny homograph riddles*. New York: Clarion Books.

SCHOOL AND TEACHERS
Lilly's Purple Plastic Purse
by Kevin Henkes
Greenwillow
1996
Ages 6–10

Lilly is one of those students who simply loves everything about school. Most of all she loves her teacher, Mr. Slinger. Everything in school is going along fine until the day Lilly brings her purple plastic purse that plays cool music. That's when the problems begin.

1. Share the first page of the book with the class. Lilly just loved everything about school. What do your students love about school? What

do they believe to be "just okay," and what would they change if they had the chance? Have the students divide a piece of paper into three sections, label each, and then tell you exactly what they think about school. What you find out may surprise you!

2. Lilly just adored Mr. Slinger. Allow your children to work individually or in groups to make a composite of the perfect teacher. If done individually, identify five things that would be true about the perfect teacher and five that the perfect teacher would never, never do. If working in a group of three or four, there can be ideas offered by each member of the group, however, the group must come to some consensus (those things everybody can agree upon). This requires more negotiation and will not work well with younger children who feel strongly that the only right ideas are their own.

3. Mr. Slinger's class had a "Lightbulb Lab" where wonderful ideas were born. Create a special place in your classroom where children can create and develop their own ideas. It can also serve as a great place to go for one-on-one instruction, as well as a small group project area. Some of the more easily distracted members of your class may find they do their best work in the Lightbulb Lab.

4. Have any of your students ever been in trouble at school as Lilly was? Give children the opportunity to talk, draw, or write about a time they got in trouble at school. Most children will have an experience they will eagerly want to share.

5. This book serves as an excellent introduction to designing classroom rules. As the teacher, you can certainly select and "tell" the rules, but we all know children will be more apt to follow the rules they create. Read this story and allow the children to identify some rules every classroom should have and then add to the list. Post these in your classroom.

6. Lilly's purse held something very special to her—movie star sunglasses that Grammy bought her. If you could bring any one thing to school, what would your special something be?

7. Using the pattern provided (see appendix A) children can design their own special movie star sunglasses. Get out the scrap box and children will make the most amazing glasses.

8. Lilly opens her purse to find a note and a surprise from her teacher. Before reading the note to the children, have them predict what they think it will say. Students can then write a note and draw a picture of a treat they would like to receive from their teacher. Paste the note on the purple construction paper purse the children can easily make with or without the use of a pattern. Place these purses on the bulletin board entitled "Notes from the Teacher."

Other Related Books:

Havill, J. (1999). *Jamaica and the substitute teacher*. Boston: Houghton Mifflin.

Henkes, K. (1996). *Chrysanthemum*. New York: Mulberry.

~~~

SCHOOL AND TEACHERS
Teacher from the Black Lagoon
by Mike Thaler
Scholastic Books
1989
Ages 6–11

The first day of school can be filled with anxiety. Just thinking about it and what your teacher might be like is enough to make you more than nervous. That's what happens to the boy in this story who imagines the worst about his teacher. Good thing it's only a terrible dream!

1. It's a great book to start off the year in your classroom. Are you a real monster? with claws? breathing fire? swallowing children with one gulp? Before the children really find out all about you, let them describe the "perfect teacher." Place students into groups of four and encourage the use of a puzzle graphic organizer to collect their thoughts (see appendix A). Each child gets one piece of the puzzle and should write thoughts about what makes a perfect teacher. After each child finishes, the puzzle is assembled and ideas are shared. The recorder of the group will write all the ideas (no duplication) in the center of the puzzle. These group identified characteristics are then shared with the class and the teacher. Here's the teacher's big chance to see how they measure up to the students' perceptions of a "perfect teacher" and why some of their requests (like "never gives homework") just won't be possible. Everyone gets a good laugh and this activity works well to minimize teacher and student anxiety, as well as getting kids to work together on a fun project on the very first day of school.

2. Using the newspaper, examine want ads. What kinds of things are important to include? Encourage students to write a good want ad for the "perfect teacher" remembering they only have $_____ and the add will cost _____ cents per word. Math skills get utilized as students learn to be concise in their descriptions. How much will your teacher ad cost to run for one day, three days, seven days? There

is a special promotion giving you the second week for one-half price. How much will the ad cost to run for two weeks?

3. Allow children the opportunity to get to know you as a person—not just their teacher. Using the alphabet as the pattern, make a book, "The ABC's of Ms./Mr. _____". For each letter of the alphabet, tell something abut yourself (A—I grew up in Arizona; B—I have one brother. His name is Jerry, etc.). Make it a class project with everyone making his/her own book. It's a great ice breaker at the beginning of the year for you and your students and a wonderful way for even the most quiet child to share personal information. And, of course, it helps your class see you as more than just "the teacher!"

Other Related Books:

Allard, H. (1985). *Miss Nelson is missing!* Boston: Houghton Mifflin.

Dakos, K. (1996). *The goof who invented homework: And other school poems*. New York: Dial.

Lasky, K. (1996). *Lunch bunnies*. Boston: Little, Brown.

O'Malley, K. (1996). *Miss Malarkey doesn't live in room 10*. New York: Walker & Co.

SCHOOL AND TEACHERS
Thank You, Mr. Falker
by Patricia Polacco
Philomel Books
1998
All Ages

It wasn't until Patricia Polacco was in fifth grade that a teacher discovered her reading problem and was able to help her discover the magic of books and the printed word. This book is a powerful testimonial to the importance of teachers and the long remembered role they play in the lives of their students.

1. Discuss with the children in your class the many things they are especially good at. Are there things that are not as easy for you? Discuss. Each of us can make a list in each category and it might help your students "get into" the discussion if you begin with yourself. Children will quickly understand that the largest and the smallest, the oldest and the youngest, the richest and the poorest have things we excel in and other things we continue to work at day after day after day.

2. Show children how much growth they make during the year they spend with you. Sometimes, it's hard to see the changes over time unless we pay special attention to them. At the beginning of the year give each child a manila folder. Encourage them to decorate it any way they'd like to, but all title it, "Look How I've Grown." Inside they will paste a sheet you have made that helps them chart their progress, improvements, strengths, and areas they continue to work on. Younger children would enjoy a page that is divided into boxes so that they may document their growth through illustrations.

3. As students begin the school year, encourage them to think of the significant teachers in their lives—the ones they remember because they recognized your strengths, made you work harder than you thought you could, encouraged you when you stopped wanting to try, or just cared and made you feel like the important person you are. Write a thank you note to that teacher to tell him/her what you feel and how they made an impact on your life.

Other Related Books:

Ashley, B. (1995). *Cleversticks*. New York: Random House.
Cazat, D. (1990). *Never spit on your shoes*. New York: Orchard
Duffey, B. (1999). *How to be cool in the third grade*. New York: Puffin.
Hurwitz, J. (1989). *Russell Sprouts*. New York: Viking Press.
Pulver, R. (1992) *Nobody's Mother is in second grade*. New York: Dial
Books for Young Readers.

~~~

SCHOOL AND TEACHERS
Dear Mr. Blueberry
by Simon James
Margaret McElderry Books
1991
Ages 5 and up

While on a summer vacation, Emily writes to her teacher for advice about a whale living in her garden pond! Throughout their letter writing, Emily learns about whales and Mr. Blueberry learns about imagination, faith, and friendship.

1. Many of the events in the story came from Emily's imagination. To reinforce the discrimination of real and make believe, distribute several index cards to each student and ask them to write a real or make believe sentence on each. Collect all cards and place them in a bag.

As students draw a card, they should read it to the class and categorize it as real or make-believe.

2. Using this story format as the pattern, pair each child with a partner. One member of the team will be the imaginative child and the other Mr. or Mrs. _____(students may use their last name rather than Blueberry). The imaginative child will write a letter telling of a make-believe situation and ask a question. Mr./Mrs. _____ will write back as the adult did in the book. The pairs of students can correspond with each other for several days and then their letters can be made into a book. Give it a title and put it in the classroom library so all can "check it out"!

3. Keep in touch with your students over the summer vacation with a postcard writing activity. As an end of the year gift, give each child a postcard that has your address pre-printed on it. Just as Emily wrote to her teacher, so can your students. Encourage them to share some of the fun and excitement of their summer with you. You, of course, can write back. If you feel this is a lot of writing for you, then write one message with a fine tip black marker starting with Dear (omit name). Take this to your nearest copy center to have it copied on cardstock. Fill in individual student names with that same fine tip black marker and it will look just like a personalized, hand written note. Add a stamp and, Viola, you can communicate with your 20 plus students as simply as communicating with one!

Other Related Books:

Border, L. (1999). *Good luck, Mrs. K.* New York: Margaret McElderry Books.

Brown, M. (1987). *Arthur's teacher trouble.* New York: Little Brown & Company.

Houston, G. (1992). *My great-aunt Arizona.* New York: HarperCollins.

Krensky, S. (1996). *My teacher's secret life.* New York: Simon & Schuster.

~~~

FAIRY AND TALL TALES
Folks Call Me Appleseed John
by Andrew Glass
Doubleday
1998
Ages 7–11

Johnny Appleseed is not only a wonderful tale but he, the real John Chapman, was a wonderful storyteller, and this book describes both the man and his humor. This special independent man and American hero's favorite story was about his brother Nathaniel and their adventures in western Pennsylvania. That story and the pioneer spirit come alive in this new book!

1. Tall tales are based on exaggeration. Explore the idea of blowing something way out of proportion by asking each of your students to write one true fact about themselves and then rewrite it using exaggeration. Vote on the best exaggeration in your class. This is one time when telling tales is recommended!

2. Why not build your own tall tales? Using four containers (shoe boxes, coffee cans, envelopes, etc.) decorate and label each with the headings 1) animal names, 2) natural features, 3) a tall tale character; and 4) character trait or skill. Each child contributes one slip of paper to each can with his/her own response to each category. Now the fun begins. Mix the cans well and everyone selects one slip of paper from each can. This will be the basis for your writing activity as you create your own new, original, and quite unique tall tale.

3. Help tall tales come to life in your classroom by creating a "Hall of Tall Tale Characters" (a spin off on Disney's Hall of Presidents). Each student must read and learn about a selected tall tale character. Now make some simple costumes and "become" the tall tale character or the wife, son, or daughter of that character.

4. Tall tales invite us into the lives of characters sometimes larger than life. Invite your class to follow up their study of tall tales with learning about the lives of real life characters through reading biographies. May 10 is National Biography Day—a perfect time to explore our own lives. Using the alphabet as your format, write and illustrate a book telling about yourself. Photos also add to your "tell all biography." Share your "best-seller" with your students and let the fun begin as they then begin to tell about themselves in their own "ABC About Me" books.

5. Another variety of biography exploration is to offer your class certain criteria to follow and things they must include in their books. These might include information about yourself as a baby, your family, vacations you have gone on, what you like to do for fun, your friends, what you are good at, not so good at, things you collect, most memorable time, etc. Also, you can depict biographical events through a Personal Time Line. Cut a 12 x 18" piece of paper in half lengthwise. Fold each piece into accordion folds (like you are making a fan) so that each equals 6 segments. Glue together the two 6 segment pieces to equal 12 continuous segments and write and draw about you! There's plenty to show and 12 segments in which to show it!

Other Related Books:

Kellogg, S. (1996). *I was born about 10,000 years ago*. New York: Morrow.

Pinkney, A. (1996). *Bill Pickett: Rodeo-ridin' cowboy*. New York: Harcourt Brace.

Sloat, T. (1997). *Sody Sallyratus*. New York: Dutton.

Spurr, E. (1997). *The long, long letter*. New York: Disney.

Wood, A. (1996). *The Bunyans*. New York: Blue Sky Press.

~~~~~

FAIRY AND TALL TALES
William the Curious, Knight of the Water Lilies
by Charles Santore
Random House
1997
Ages 6–11

Insisting on perfection, the queen decrees that anything even slightly damaged be thrown out of the castle window and into the moat, the home of frog William. Quite displeased (and now much more crowded), William dares to ask the queen why minor imperfections are so terrible. The story is a modern fairy tale with a modern message—save the environment including the moat!

1. Why not "hop" into recycling this spring as Earth Day rolls around in April. A perfect bulletin board would be to provide materials for each child to make a lily pad and water lily. On the flower write his/her name and on the lily pad individual suggestions about making our world better, cleaner, and more ecologically sound.

2. An Imperfect Scavenger Hunt. To remind students of the Three R's of Trash—Recycle, Reduce, and Reuse, send each child home with the task of locating three objects around the house that have imperfections. Investigate certain questions about these objects. Do they still work? Do the imperfections stop them from working or being useful? If so, can they be fixed? Before throwing them away, can they be used in any other way?

3. What do we mean by the old adage "One man's trash is another man's treasure?" Discuss this with your class and prepare to have a treasure exchange in your classroom to demonstrate the meaning of this old adage. Begin with writing a letter to families about your unit on recycling. Encourage each parent to send in one toy, book,

puzzle, or game their family is tired of or has outgrown but is one which they believe someone in your class might still enjoy. As each student brings in a "slightly used, but still good" treasure, they receive a paper water lily with a number on it. On the day of the big exchange, numbers are drawn to select the order; and when your number is called, you may claim a treasure.

Other Related Books:

Egielski, R. (1997). *The gingerbread boy*. New York: HarperCollins.

Ernst, L. C. (1995). *Little red riding hood: A newfangled prairie tale*. New York: Simon & Schuster.

Quindlen, K. (1997). *Happily ever after*. New York: Viking.

FAIRY AND TALL TALES
Fanny's Dream
by Carolyn Buehner
Illustrated by Mark Buehner
Dial
1996
Ages 7 and up

Fanny Agnes always believed that she would marry a handsome prince. She waited for her fairy godmother to come, but Hebner Jensen showed up instead. He wasn't quite the Prince Charming she had anticipated, but…

1. Share a more traditional version of Cinderella with the students. What are the elements which make this a fairy tale? Now read *Fanny's Dream* and discuss whether it has the same elements as the original story. Is it also a fairy tale? Discuss how the stories are alike and different. Using a Venn Diagram students can identify elements of Cinderella in one circle, elements specific to Fanny in the other circle, and in the center which overlaps include the similarities. Allow students to in some way, compare the two characters (Cinderella and Fanny). Making a character web for each works well.

2. Fanny had a dream—it just didn't turn out exactly as she thought it would. Allow students to write about a dream they had that turned out differently than they had hoped. Discuss how sometimes the way dreams turn out is better than what they originally hoped for. Do we always know what is best for us?

3. Students will enjoy researching other famous Americans (men and

women) who had a dream and achieved that dream. What did they dream for and hope to achieve. How did they go about reaching their dream?

4. Rewrite the story from Hebner Jensen's point of view. How does the author's perspective affect the way the story is told?

5. Write a sequel to the Fanny and Hebner story. What does their future hold? Will they continue to be happy? What about their careers? Their children?

6. Students can rewrite their own version of Cinderella, putting themselves and other friends and family in the characters' roles. The rewrite should reflect their own personality and life.

Other Related Books:

Ada, A. F. (1998). *Yours truly, Goldilocks*. New York: Atheneum.

Asch, F. (1998). *Ziggy Piggy: And the three little pigs*. Toronto, ON, Canada: Kids Can.

Bailey, L. (1997). *Gordon Loggins and the 3 bears*. Toronto, ON, Canada: Kids Can.

Ketteman, H. (1997). *Bubba the cowboy prince: A fractured Texas tale*. New York: Scholastic.

Lowell, S. (1997). *Little red cowboy hat*. New York: Henry Holt.

THEME: FAIRY AND TALL TALES
Rapunzel, A Happenin' Rap
by David Vozar
Illustrated by Betsy Levin
Doubleday
1998
Ages 7–12

The infectious rap beat of this retelling of an old and favorite classic is perfect for reading aloud. Your class will love the rhythm and rhyme as well as the surprises this book holds from start to finish.

1. Use this story as a springboard to creating other "What if…" stories. What if the three bears had lived in the year 2020? What if Rapunzel had very short hair? What if the frog prince had been the hyena prince? Rewrite the story with a twist.

2. Encourage children to use a story such as this one with great dialogue to write their own Readers' Theater. Remember, in Readers'

Theater there are no props, costumes, or memorized lines. Children read parts much like an old radio show. Their use of good voice and expression is what takes the audience on an enjoyable journey. Teach your class about pausing at appropriate times, phrasing, tone, and voice inflection, which will all make for a great performance. Identify characters (remember, not every child has to have a part) and, of course, it is always best to have a narrator to carry the story from one scene to the next. After reading the story aloud, allow the students to decide how they will retell the story without feeling the pressure of using the author's exact words.

     Note: You may choose to use longer chapter books for this activity. Simply allow children to select a scene or chapter which they would most like to interpret through Readers' Theater.

3. Take any fairy tale classic and retell it with a new twist. Who says Little Red has to walk to Gramma's house and that she has to travel through the woods. Change the characters, settings, and even the title. See what your students can create. They may become the folk tales of tomorrow.

4. Create a fairy tale museum. Ask each child to select a fairy tale and share it with you but no one else. Control the selections so that there are no duplicates. Now the class can create a Fairy Tale Museum in your classroom. Each child will collect artifacts to identify the fairy tale he/she has selected. They will display these items at a numbered station. After all displays are complete, each child will try to guess the fairy tale simply by the items collected and displayed. For instance, if I were to display a few pieces of straw, a few candy gold coins, and a little troll doll, which fairy tell would I be representing? The creativity of your class will astound you!

Other Related Books:

Kellogg, S. (1997). *The three little pigs*. New York: Morrow.

Ray, J. (1996). *The twelve dancing princesses*. New York: Dutton.

Thaler, M. (1997). *Cinderella bigfoot*. New York: Scholastic

Yolen, J. (1997). *Twelve impossible things before breakfast*. San Diego: Harcourt Brace.

Yolen, J. (1998). *King long shanks*. New York: Scholastic.

JUST FOR THE FUN OF IT
The Fixits
by Anne Mazer
Illustrated by Paul Meisel
Hyperion Books
1999
Ages 5–9

Michael and Augusta have broken their mother's favorite plate and must fix it before she gets home. Time to call the Fixits, a team who is better at causing accidents than fixing them. As they destroy everything they touch, they generate a wild romp and lots of laughter.

1. In the story, the Fixits continually say, "Accidents happen. We can fix it." Encourage children to tell of an accident that happened in which they were involved. Could it be "fixed"?

2. Many people work in a "fix-it" occupation (plumber, electrician, tailor, etc.) Brainstorm with your class to see how many "fix-it occupations" you can identify. Make a group list and allow children to illustrate each occupation.

3. Think about a time when you broke something. Write a story to tell what the Fixits did when they arrived at your house.

4. Allow children to closely examine the picture near the end of the story that shows the house when mother arrived home. Many objects are incorrectly placed in the house (typewriter on the wall, a door turned sideways, a bathtub on the roof. Have the children draw their house as it really appears but ask them to make a few mistakes in placing some of the objects just as the Fixits did.

5. Not all problems are mechanical in nature. Select someone in your class to be Mr. or Ms. Fixit. During the school day, it will be their job to handle the problems that come up. What will they suggest when someone looses his/her lunch money, a child forgets her math homework, someone is unkind to a child, or the class gets too noisy? Let a child in your class feel very special as the Mr./Ms. Fixit of the Day!

Other Related Books:

Blume, J. (1990). *Fudge a mania*. New York: E.P. Dutton.
Hurwitz, J. (1983). *Rip-roaring Russell*. New York: William Morrow.
Parish, P. (1999). *Amelia Bedelia*. New York: Harperfestival.
Simont, M. (1996). *My Brother, Ant*. New York: Viking.

JUST FOR THE FUN OF IT
Grandpa's Teeth
by Rod Clement
HarperCollins
1998
Ages 5 and up

It's a "disthaster" when Grandpa's false teeth are stolen and every-one in town is a suspect! The only way to prove your innocence is by smiling. Will grandpa find his teeth? Who has taken them? This book will keep readers giggling and grinning.

1. This book is a great springboard into your dental health unit. Dis-cuss ways to keep teeth strong and healthy. Make a bulletin board or chart that is titled, "Grandpa says" and list all the important ele-ments of good dental health.

2. The series of events in this story can lead to an activity that makes practicing sequencing of events really fun! The activity called "Film Making" will use the film-frames template found in appendix A. Duplicate these frames so that each student gets three sheets. The directions are as follows:

    Frame 1:   Print the Title of the Book, Author, and Illustrator (child uses his/her own name here).

    Frames 2, 4,   Select three favorite scenes from the story. Illustrate
    and 6:   them in sequential order (one on each of the noted frames).

    Frames 3, 5,   Write _____ sentences describing the preceding scene
    and 7:   you choose to illustrate.

    Frame 8:   Write THE END

    Tape together all three pieces and attach them at the top to a card-board tube from a paper towel roll. Decorate the role any way you'd like.

3. Have a Greatest Smile Contest in your classroom. As a group, de-cide what makes for a great simile. Take a photo of each child in your class and proudly display on each student's locker. (NOTE: These photos can later be put to good use when students make deco-rative picture frames and include the photo with it as a holiday gift.) Give the students one week to examine the photos and compare them to the criteria identified by the class. Voting can occur with a secret ballot that the students can count, tally, and graph. Have a "Smile Party" to announce the winner of The Greatest Smile Con-test and celebrate good dental health.

4. In this story, everyone in town smiled all the time (even without any

reason) to verify that the teeth in their mouth were their own. Ask each student to create a list called "Ten Things That Make Me Smile" or make a similar class list with one entry from each student titled "Twenty-Two Things that Make Us Smile".

5. Imagine that you are working for a local television station and have been given the assignment of interviewing Grandpa. Select a partner. One of you will write 5 good questions you would like to ask Grandpa. The partner then writes Grandpa's answers to each of the questions. The interviewing duo will read their questions and answers to the class.

Other Related Books:

Cushman, D. (1996). *The ABC mystery*. New York: HarperCollins.

Cushman, D. (1996). *The mystery of King Karfu*. New York: HarperCollins.

Tryon, L. (1998). *Albert's Halloween: The case of the stolen pumpkins*. New York: Antheneum.

Tudor, T. (1997). *The great Corgiville kidnapping*. New York: Little Brown.

Whatley, B. (1997). *Detective Donut and the wild goose chase*. New York: HarperCollins.

~~~

JUST FOR THE FUN OF IT
Mistakes That Worked
by Charlotte Foltz Jones
Doubleday Books
1991
Ages 8–12

Many of the things we use daily in our schools and homes were discovered quite by accident. This book tells about forty of them from Levi jeans to post-it notes and popsicles.

1. Your students (and the teacher, too) will love reading about some of the entrepreneurs whose inventions can now be found in every home in America. Use this as an opportunity to explore some other inventions including the most famous and some perhaps less famous. Brainstorm with your class to create a list of inventions. Children will select the one they most want to learn about. Have each child write a report and present it to the class. As the teacher, you should give some research guidelines to help students know what kind of

information you'd like to have included such as:
- a brief background on the inventor,
- the time period during which this was being developed and when it was first marketed,
- what led up to the invention,
- a picture of the invention,
- how has the invention changed over the years.

2. Imagine you are the famous inventor you are researching. Write a letter to a friend telling about the discovery you are about to unveil to the world.
3. Create an invention time line in your class where students will organize their selected inventions from the earliest developed to the most recent.
4. Have an "Invention Convention." Let the creative juices of your students flow! Ask them to consider an invention not yet made that they would like to see created. What would it do? What would it be called? How would it be made? Where would you buy it? What would it look like?
5. Write a newspaper article making front page news about this new invention. Remember the five Ws of good journalistic reporting: who, what, when, where, and why. Be sure to include these in your piece that tells John Q. Public what he is clamoring to know about this newsbreaking event.

Other Related Books:

Brown, A. E (compiler). (1976). *Absolutely mad inventions*. Mineola, NY: Dove Publishers.

Hewitt, S. (1997). *The things we use (Have you noticed)*. Austin, TX: Raintree, Steck, and Vaughn.

Jacobs, D. (1995). *What does it do?* Austin, TX: Raintree, Steck, and Vaughn.

Jones, C. F. (1998). *Accidents may happen*. New York: Bantam Doubleday.

Parker, S. (1995). *53 1/2 things that changed the world: And some that didn't*. Brookfield, CT: Millbrook.

Appendix A

Templates, Patterns, and Support for Literature Extensions

All About Me Chart

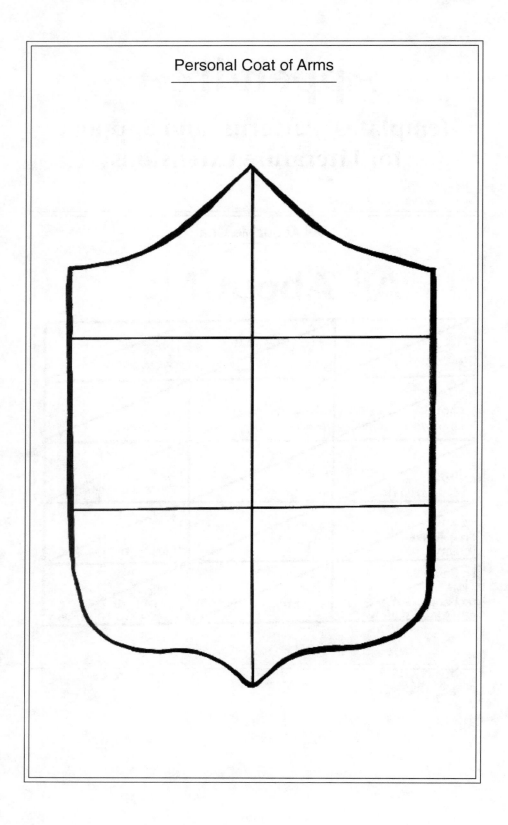

Personal Coat of Arms

The Solutions Chart

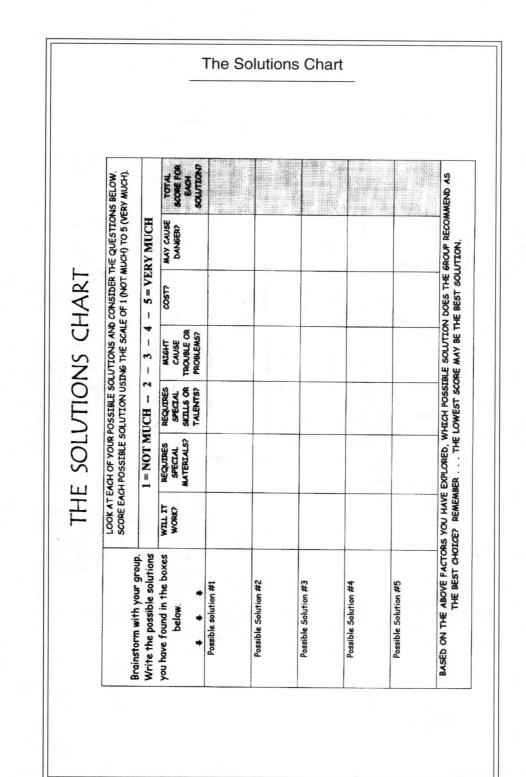

THE SOLUTIONS CHART

LOOK AT EACH OF YOUR POSSIBLE SOLUTIONS AND CONSIDER THE QUESTIONS BELOW.
SCORE EACH POSSIBLE SOLUTION USING THE SCALE OF 1 (NOT MUCH) TO 5 (VERY MUCH).

1 = NOT MUCH – 2 – 3 – 4 – 5 = VERY MUCH

Brainstorm with your group.
Write the possible solutions
you have found in the boxes
below.

	WILL IT WORK?	REQUIRES SPECIAL MATERIALS?	REQUIRES SPECIAL SKILLS OR TALENTS?	MIGHT CAUSE TROUBLE OR PROBLEMS?	COST?	MAY CAUSE DANGER?	TOTAL SCORE FOR EACH SOLUTION?
Possible solution #1							
Possible Solution #2							
Possible Solution #3							
Possible Solution #4							
Possible Solution #5							

BASED ON THE ABOVE FACTORS YOU HAVE EXPLORED, WHICH POSSIBLE SOLUTION DOES THE GROUP RECOMMEND AS
THE BEST CHOICE? REMEMBER . . . THE LOWEST SCORE MAY BE THE BEST SOLUTION.

Movie Star Glasses

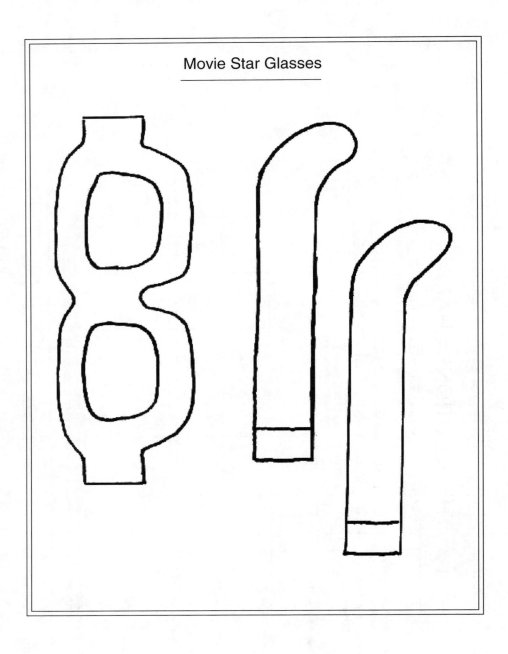

Puzzle Graphic Organizer

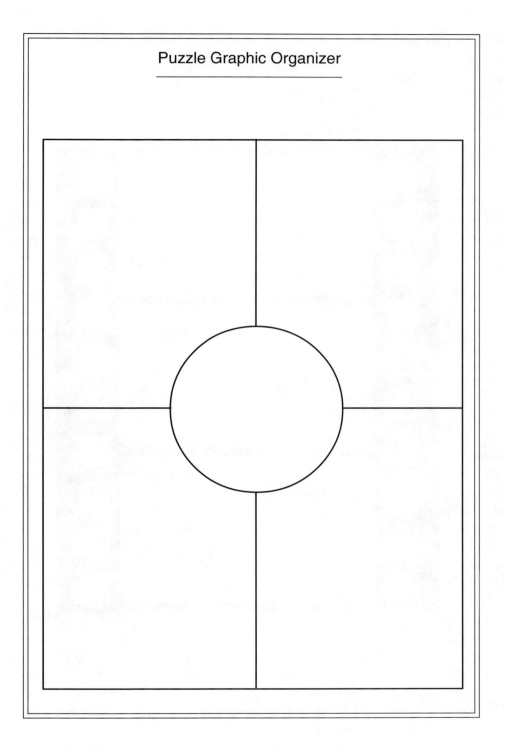

Film-Frames

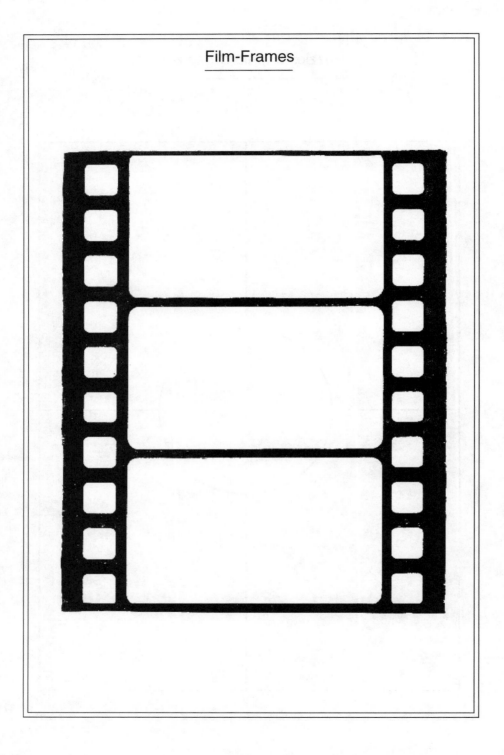

Author Index

Subject Index

About the Author

Barbara Nypaver Kupetz is an Associate Professor in the early childhood and elementary teacher preparation programs at Indiana University of Pennsylvania. There she teaches both undergraduate and graduate courses in literacy. She spent many years as an elementary and early childhood teacher and she continues to have an active presence in classrooms where she frequently can be found trying new and innovative ways to use literature. Dr. Kupetz has written numerous articles on literacy and literature and is the author of two children's books, *What's New with Mr. Pizooti?* and *Indiana County A-Z.*